ROCK N ROLL BRIDE

THE ULTIMATE GUIDE FOR ALTERNATIVE BRIDES

Kat Williams

with photography by Lisa Devlin and Lisa Jane Photography

RYLAND PETERS & SMALL

LONDON • NEW YORK

This book is dedicated to all Rock n Roll brides.
Here's to forging your own path, saying no to
ugly chair covers and finding marital bliss.

Designers
Toni Kay, Emily Breen
Jacket Design
Shauna Haider
of We are Branch
Commissioning Editor
Alice Sambrook
Head of Production
Patricia Harrington
Editorial Director
Julia Charles
Publisher
Cindy Richards
Indexer
Hilary Bird

Published in 2019 by
Ryland Peters & Small
20–21 Jockey's Fields
London WC1R 4BW
and
341 E 116th Street
New York, 10029
www.rylandpeters.com
10 9 8 7 6 5 4 3 2

Text copyright © Kat
Williams 2019
Design copyright ©
Ryland Peters & Small
2019

ISBN: 978-1-78879-065-9

A CIP record for this
book is available from
the British Library.
US Library of Congress
CIP data has been
applied for.

Printed in Slovenia

See page 204 for full
photography credits

CONTENTS

INTRODUCTION

Here's to the weirdos, the misfits, the babes who break the mould. To the brides who refuse to conform and the ones who don't want to do what's expected of them.

As a child I never dreamed about my wedding day. I didn't dress up as a bride, hang a pillowcase on the back of my head or have a scrapbook full of my future wedding plans.

As a teenager I only ever wondered who would fall in love with me, the idea of weddings, marriage and/or having kids never came into it.

My dreams were about independence, about starting my own business and living a life that made me happy. Ironically, I didn't actually start achieving these things until I met my now-husband, we got engaged and I started a blog.

Like most brides-to-be, as soon as that sparkler was on my finger I excitedly rushed out and purchased every wedding magazine I could find, and took to the internet with the conviction and motivation of a woman possessed. I wanted to absorb and learn everything and anything I could about how to plan a wedding. But what I was met with was a boring, outdated industry that only seemed to focus on tradition and big budgets.

We didn't want a big fancy wedding, we didn't want a horse and carriage or to spend a ridiculous amount of money on a car to take me five minutes down the road. I didn't want to wear a strapless, white dress and I certainly didn't want to

promise to obey my husband. We didn't really know what we wanted, but we knew that it certainly wasn't anything like that.

To me, everything I saw felt boring, antiquated and like a carbon copy of every other wedding that had come before it. Where was the fun? Where were the unique ideas? Where was the real love story of the couple committing their lives to each other? It all felt very flat.

So, in October 2007 I started my blog. Initially it was a personal diary to share our wedding plans and ideas, but fast forward to after our wedding and I realized I actually quite enjoyed this blogging thing and I didn't just want to give it all up now I was a wife. I loved connecting with like-minded people (brides-to-be and people starting out in the industry) who were also looking for something different.

Over the next few years, Rock n Roll Bride evolved from a personal blog, to a blog publishing real weddings with alternative flair that were submitted from all over the globe. I also started writing advice columns to help my readers plan their own unique celebrations. In 2010, I quit my job as a television producer to work on the website full-time, and in 2011 my husband, Gareth, did the same. Despite catering for a niche market (*Brides* magazine, we are not) it is now one of the highest trafficked wedding websites in the world.

In 2015, we launched a bi-monthly print magazine which is not only stocked in stores up and down the UK, but shipped direct to our thousands of loyal subscribers all over the world. It still blows my mind that I get to do this as a job. I'm just a punk kid from Reading with rainbow hair and one too many tattoos who's always been too stubborn to ever do anything that was expected of her.

Needless to say, the wedding industry has moved on a lot in the past 12 years, and I firmly believe (without wanting to toot my own horn too much) that Rock n Roll Bride has been a major catalyst for that change. No longer is having a DIY or budget wedding seen as a shameful thing, finding a non-traditional wedding gown is easier than ever and there are countless businesses now marketing themselves towards an alternative wedding-loving clientele.

Rock n Roll Bride is all about the charm and unique nature of ordinary people's extraordinary weddings. This book will help you navigate the muddy waters of planning a wedding that goes against the grain. It'll help you with everything from setting your theme, to finding suppliers that 'get you', dealing with difficult family dynamics and coping with the post-wedding blues. This book features gorgeous imagery to inspire you, but most importantly, it's packed with practical advice that will help you plan your wedding in your own unique way.

This book is for everyone who's ever considered themselves an outsider, a weirdo, someone who doesn't quite fit in. Being Rock 'n' Roll is not about being rebellious or even thinking of the most out-there ideas that you can, it's simply about planning a wedding that reflects you, your partner and your love.

This is about living your life on your own terms. It's about being comfortable in your own skin (or working towards getting there one day). It's about not simply rolling over and accepting things just because 'that's the way things are, dear', it's about questioning the status quo and finding your own path.

You don't have to be wacky, you don't have to be offbeat and you certainly don't have to be cool…You just have to be you.

You got this (fist bump).

the ESSENTIALS

GETTING STARTED

CONGRATULATIONS!

As a newly engaged babe, you'll likely be experiencing an intoxicating mixture of emotions right now. While everyone you speak to will helpfully remind you that this should be the happiest time in your life, you will probably soon start feeling that inevitable wave of panic: 'Oh goodness, we have so much to organize, so much to do, and so much to pay for!'

First of all, please realize that it's perfectly normal to be a little bit scared and overwhelmed at this stage. I mean, most of you reading this will never have planned a wedding before and there's a lot to get your head around.

Before we dig into the more practical advice, I want to preface by reminding you that yes, this is an important day, but also that it's just ONE DAY. Your wedding will be a wonderful celebration, and a lovely starting point for your marriage, but it will not define the rest of your life. So, if you ever find yourself falling into the trap of hyperventilating over guest lists, seating arrangements and finding that one perfect dress, always remind yourself why you're doing this in the first place.

Whenever I'm faced with an enormous task, I find it way less overwhelming if I can break it down into manageable chunks. Having an idea of your planning timeline and checklist (see pages 14–15) is a good place to begin. You don't have to do everything right away (and despite what many suppliers/vendors and magazines will tell you, if you are willing to be flexible you can TOTALLY get a lot done in a short time frame if necessary). At the end of the day, the important thing is that you end up married and get to celebrate your love in a way that feels special to you, not that you had that extravagant floral installation, that fireworks went off at the exact moment you said 'I do' or that everyone else has since called it THE BEST DAY EVER.

PLANNING TIMELINE & CHECKLIST

Whether you have three years or three weeks to plan your wedding, keeping organized is vital. Based on (the average) 12–18-month engagement, this is a general guideline of what you can expect to do and when. Of course, lots of these elements are optional, and if your time frame is much shorter, or you are DIYing rather than buying, just adapt it to suit your needs.

AS SOON AS YOU GET ENGAGED
- ☐ Set your priorities and begin discussing your theme
- ☐ Set the budget

12-18 MONTHS
- ☐ Set your date
- ☐ Find and book your venue
- ☐ Start researching suppliers/vendors

10-12 MONTHS
- ☐ Start to compile the guest list
- ☐ Send your Save the Dates
- ☐ Buy wedding insurance
- ☐ Choose your bridal party
- ☐ Start researching your outfit and visiting bridal boutiques to try things on!
- ☐ Book a photographer and/or videographer
- ☐ Book a wedding planner/day of-coordinator
- ☐ Book a caterer

8-10 MONTHS
- ☐ Finalize your guest list
- ☐ Book your ceremony/officiant
- ☐ Book musicians/entertainment
- ☐ Book transport

- ☐ Book a hair and make-up artist
- ☐ Book any large rentals such as chairs, tables, marquee etc.
- ☐ Book a florist
- ☐ Order your cake
- ☐ Start looking for and order your dress
- ☐ Think about the hen/bachelorette party/bridal shower and discuss with your maid of honour

6-8 MONTHS
- ☐ Research and book your honeymoon
- ☐ Set up a gift list/wedding registry
- ☐ Start researching wedding party outfits
- ☐ Start your DIY projects
- ☐ Order or make invitations
- ☐ Send out invitations

4-6 MONTHS
- ☐ Have a hair and make-up trial
- ☐ Buy rings
- ☐ Give notice/arrange for the banns to be read

2-4 MONTHS
- ☐ Collect RSVPs
- ☐ Organize the seating plan
- ☐ Write your vows

- ☐ Decide on ceremony music and readings
- ☐ Create your wedding day programmes
- ☐ Finalize wedding party outfits
- ☐ Buy your shoes and accessories
- ☐ Create the running order of your day and send it to all your suppliers/vendors
- ☐ Have an engagement shoot with your photographer
- ☐ Have a tasting with your caterers and set the menu

1–2 MONTHS

- ☐ Have the hen/bachelorette party or bridal shower
- ☐ Buy some thank-you gifts for your parents and the wedding party
- ☐ Have your final dress fitting (make sure you've bought some appropriate underwear!)
- ☐ Call all your suppliers/vendors and confirm dates, times and locations
- ☐ Chase any guests who haven't RSVP'd

2–4 WEEKS

- ☐ Give final guest numbers to your caterer
- ☐ Get a final haircut and colour
- ☐ Organize music playlist(s)
- ☐ Confirm ceremony arrangements

1–2 WEEKS

- ☐ Make final payments to your suppliers/vendors
- ☐ Practice your vows
- ☐ Give ceremony readers their scripts
- ☐ Do some pre-wedding pampering!
- ☐ Finalize the seating plan
- ☐ Finish all your DIY projects
- ☐ Pick up your dress
- ☐ Confirm honeymoon arrangements and pack

THE DAY BEFORE

- ☐ Go to your venue to set up the décor (or instruct your day-of coordinator how to do this)
- ☐ Give rings to the best man

ON THE DAY

- ☐ Keep calm and enjoy your day!

AFTER THE WEDDING

If you've changed your name be sure to let everyone know:

- ☐ Your employer
- ☐ Your bank
- ☐ Your landlord or mortgage company
- ☐ Any credit card companies
- ☐ Utility services such as gas, water, electricity
- ☐ Your local authority
- ☐ The police (if you have any criminal actions against you)
- ☐ Passport Office (if you choose to apply for a new passport right away – you can still travel on your old passport even if you legally change your name. You just need to make sure you book your tickets in your maiden name!)
- ☐ DVLA/DMV
- ☐ Any breakdown organizations
- ☐ Telephone/Internet provider
- ☐ Doctor
- ☐ Dentist
- ☐ Vets
- ☐ TV licence office (if applicable)
- ☐ School/college/university

- ☐ Send thank-you cards
- ☐ Enjoy married life

SETTING YOUR PRIORITIES & BUDGETING

While crunching numbers is obviously not the most enjoyable part of any task, having a strong grasp of your finances will make things much less stressful overall. It will help you keep things in perspective and will protect your future. Yes, you could charge everything to a credit card and worry about it later, but you probably don't want to start married life with a mountain of debt.

My advice is to set your own personal priories. Sit down and look at everything you think you might need for a wedding and work out which things are the most important to you and which things you can do without. Categorize them into the following:

1. THE NON-NEGOTIABLES The things you definitely want and are willing to spend the most on. Look at what things in life are most important to you as individuals and as a couple outside of the wedding bubble.

2. THE THINGS YOU WANT BUT CAN BE FLEXIBLE ABOUT With some clever planning, you can save money on some things by going a less traditional route, calling in favours or getting your DIY on. See pages 18–19 for more ideas on making your budget stretch further.

3. THE THINGS YOU DON'T CARE ABOUT There are so many add-ons when it comes to weddings. If you don't care about something, then go right ahead and scrap it.

There is no right or wrong answer when it comes to categorizing your priorities – if you want to spend more on your dream gown and an incredible location, but you don't care about carrying a bouquet made from store-bought flowers or having a Spotify playlist instead of a band, then you do that!

As a side note, if your parents are involved in the planning (especially if they're contributing financially) it's nice to ask them about their priorities too. A wedding is usually a day for celebrating with family, and while a traditional church ceremony might mean nothing to you, perhaps it's something your mother has always dreamed of. Compromise is key here. Getting everything exactly as you want it is not realistic in many families, so by listing your complete non-negotiables early on, you can then work out what you can be more flexible on.

You should also think about how much you actually want to spend. Just because you can afford a more expensive wedding doesn't mean you have to spend everything you have on it. It might be better to save a little nest egg for starting married life with.

Below is a breakdown of the percentage of your budget you should be expecting to allocate for each key element. Obviously, this is completely flexible and you should adapt it to fit in with your own specific priorities. However, what this will give you is a good starting point.

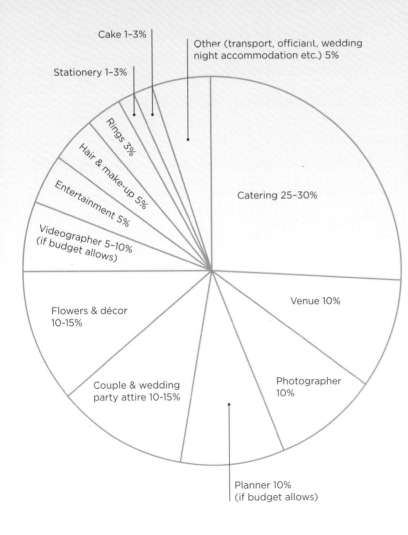

Cake 1–3%

Stationery 1–3%

Rings 3%

Hair & make-up 5%

Entertainment 5%

Videographer 5–10%
(if budget allows)

Other (transport, officiant, wedding night accommodation etc.) 5%

Catering 25–30%

Venue 10%

Flowers & décor
10–15%

Photographer
10%

Couple & wedding
party attire 10-15%

Planner 10%
(if budget allows)

MAKING YOUR BUDGET STRETCH FURTHER

Whether you have a little or a lot to spend, I'm yet to meet a couple who didn't want to make their budget stretch as far as possible.

THE CEREMONY

The ceremony is undoubtedly the most important part of any wedding and is actually the only thing you HAVE to do in order to get married. Rather than pay extra to have a registrar come out to your venue, the cheapest way to do it is to hold a short ceremony with a few witnesses at your local register office (in the UK at least two are required and in the US it varies from state to state). In England and Wales, usually notice must be given at least 28 days in advance of the wedding. Couples pay a deposit each when they give notice, a combined fee to register the marriage afterwards and a small amount to purchase the marriage certificate, which is needed to prove marital status in the future. A register office ceremony will be a short exchange of formal wording, papers will be signed and voilà, you are married!

THE VENUE

The venue will often be one of the single biggest costs of any wedding. If you want to save cash, think outside the box and don't be afraid to look beyond places specifically listed as wedding venues. While having a space that does weddings day-in-day-out will undoubtedly have its advantages (a dedicated, experienced team to help you and everything you need in one place) you can save a lot if you go for somewhere more unusual. This is not ALWAYS the case though, so be sure to ask any venue what's included (and not included!) in the hire price. If you are renting a field to put a tipi in, for example, you will probably also need to bring in bathrooms, kitchen facilities, maybe even a generator for power. This can all add up and actually make it a much more expensive – and stressful – option!

ALTERNATIVE OPTIONS Pubs, restaurants, your favourite local café, warehouses, lofts, private homes, your own back garden, farms, museums, cinemas, music venues, studio spaces, council buildings, village halls, community centres.

THE DRESS

If you don't want to spend a lot on your outfit, head to a high street or shopping mall! Many general clothing retailers now offer affordable wedding collections including ASOS, Whistles, Needle and Thread, ModCloth, BHLDN and Reformation. Buying second-hand is also a great way to save money. Well-established charity shops such as Oxfam and Barnardos have dedicated wedding dress shops. Websites like stillwhite.co.uk, preownedweddingdresses.com and good old eBay are also great places to find past-brides selling their dresses.

DÉCOR & STATIONERY

If you're a DIY queen, making the décor and stationery yourself can certainly save you cash, but keep an eye on the budget. If you're not careful, you can end up going overboard and spending way more than you originally intended.

CAKE

Having a dessert table with cakes made by your guests is an increasingly popular option. You could even host your very own Bake Off and give a prize for the best one!

ALTERNATIVE OPTIONS Make your own cake or decorate a store-bought one. Or choose donuts, pies, a cheese tower or cupcakes.

FLOWERS

Flowers can be one of the costliest parts of décor so if they aren't that important to you, there are many ways to save on them.

ALTERNATIVE OPTIONS Visit a flower market the day before or use a wholesaler. Purchase supermarket/grocery store flowers, dried flowers, silk or paper flowers.

FOOD & DRINK

As well as the venue, catering is often one of the bigger costs at a wedding. Remember, the more guests you have, the more food and drink you'll need, so the easiest way to save money overall is to invite less people. Many caterers will try to work with your budget and offer cheaper alternatives, but usually a formal sit-down meal will be one of the most expensive options.

Buying alcohol in bulk yourselves, whether that be taking advantage of seasonal offers in supermarkets/grocery stores, or by doing a booze cruise abroad, can save you a packet. But make sure you check if your venue charges corkage as this could really scupper your plans and actually make it amore expensive in the end!

ALTERNATIVE OPTIONS BBQ/cookout, finger buffet, afternoon tea, food trucks, pot luck (ask guests to bring a dish instead of a gift), pizza delivery, self-catered.

FINDING YOUR SUPPLIERS

Once you've got your ideas in place, it's time to start looking for the people who will help you make them a reality. The timeline (see pages 14–15) will give you an idea of who needs to be booked and when. Remember that some of the most popular suppliers/vendors can get booked up over a year in advance. I don't say this to scare you, but obviously a photographer can only shoot one wedding a day and many venues only host one event per day, so if you're getting married on a Saturday in high season you might want to start sending out those enquiries sooner rather than later.

WHERE TO START

Wedding blogs and magazines are great places to begin looking for suppliers/vendors and there are also lots of online directories available. However, you should still do your own research after you've found someone you like the look of. Google them, read reviews and ask to see lots of examples of their past work. Stories of suppliers not delivering what they promised are thankfully rare, but they do happen. Another great way to find suppliers is to ask any recently married friends for recommendations.

GOING RATES

It's a good idea to compare the rates and price offerings of a few different options. It's typically true that you get what you pay for, however sometimes a supplier/vendor may charge way more or way less than the average going rate. This doesn't automatically mean that they're better or worse, and while you don't want to choose someone just because they're the cheapest (in fact, someone surprisingly cheap tends to be a warning sign!), price can be a good indicator of a suppliers/vendors level of experience or how well established they are in their particular industry. Most suppliers/vendors of a similar experience, based in a similar location should be charging somewhere in the region of the same rates.

READ THE SMALL PRINT

Finally, it is VITAL that you sign a contract with all your suppliers/vendors, especially ones that will be there with you on the day (venue, photographer, videographer, caterers etc.). A contract protects both parties and will lay out clearly what you can expect and what happens if something goes wrong (for example your photographer gets sick and can't shoot your wedding). Of course, you can't be covered against literally every eventuality (this is why wedding insurance is important) but a contract gives you the best possible protection. Be sure to read contracts thoroughly before you sign and ask for clarification if something doesn't make sense. See pages 22–23 for guidance.

QUESTIONS TO ASK YOUR KEY SUPPLIERS/VENDORS

Venue

- What is your cancellation policy (if either party has to cancel)?
- What is included in the price and what do we have to pay extra for? (Tables, chairs, crockery, linens etc.)
- Is VAT/sales tax included in the price?
- What kind of insurance do you have and do we need to get our own?
- Can we bring in our own alcohol and if so, do you charge a corkage fee?
- Is photography permitted throughout?
- Will we have the venue exclusively or will it be open to the public or have other events going on at the same time?
- Is there anything that is not permitted, such as candles or hanging things from walls?
- How early can we get in to set up and when do we need to be cleared out by?
- Do you have accommodation options or suggestions for our guests?
- What time does the wedding have to end and what's your policy on loud music?
- Can we have a band/other entertainment?
- Who is our venue contact in the run up and on the day?
- How many guests can we invite?

Photographer

- Do you have public liability insurance?
- What equipment do you use? (Pro-tip: The brand of camera doesn't matter; nor does the number of fancy lenses they have. What does matter is how prepared they are and that they have backups if things break on the day. It's also worth asking whether their camera is full-frame or cropped sensor. A full-frame camera is preferable. If you're getting married in winter they may need to use flash, so ask if they have one and to see past-examples of their winter wedding photography.)
- Will we have an engagement shoot?
- How many hours of coverage do we get on the day?
- Will there be lots of posing or do you just capture things as they happen?
- Do you do group shots? How many do you recommend?
- Do we do a portrait shoot on the day? When do you recommend this happens and how long will it take?
- Is there anything not included in your package that we might have to pay extra for?

- Are your travel expenses included in the price?

- Do we need to feed you on the day?

- What do you need from us before the wedding, i.e. a must-have photo list or a group shot list?

- What happens if you get sick or for some reason can't be there on the day?

- How long will it take for us to get our photos back, how are the images delivered and how many images can we expect?

- Will all the photos be fully edited? Do we have to pay extra for any post-production/ retouching?

- Do we get an album?

- What are the costs for ordering additional prints or albums?

Caterer

- Have you catered a wedding at our venue before? Are you aware of their set up?

- Do you have a licence to prove you meet Food Standards Agency/FDA regulations?

- Do you have public liability insurance?

- Given our budget, number of guests and wedding style, what food options do you recommend?

- Is VAT/sales tax included in the price?

- Do you offer options for guests with dietary requirements or allergies?

- Does the price include a wait staff service or do we need to arrange this separately?

- Do you offer cutlery/crockery/glass hire packages or do we need to arrange this separately?

- How much do you charge for supplier/vendor meals? What do they get served?

- How much do you charge for children's meals?

- Do you offer a menu tasting and what's the charge for this?

- When do you need our final guest count by?

THE
GUEST LIST

Ahh, the guest list – after the budget this is probably the area that gives most couples the biggest headache. As with everything wedding related, there is no definitive right or wrong way to do this, but I suggest this method: Sit down with your fiancé and write down the names of everyone you want to invite, categorized as A, B or C-list guests. If you want both your parents to be involved, you can ask them to do the same and then compare lists.

THE A LIST are the non-negotiables, in other words, the people you definitely want to invite – your immediate family and your best friends. These are the people to send your Save the Dates to as soon as you have it fixed.

THE B LIST are backups who you'll invite if someone from the A-list can't make it. Co-workers would probably be on this list, and family and friends that you don't see as often.

THE C LIST are the people you'll only invite to the evening party (if you're having one). Co-workers you are less close to, the acquaintances who you chat to at the pub, the guy your dad plays golf with, your friends from school who you only catch up with at Christmas.

On average approximately, 20 per cent of your A-list guests will not be able to make it, so be sure to send out your Save the Dates and then invitations in plenty of time. No one wants to get a last-minute invite and realize they were a backup! I'd suggest sending your invites out around 6-8 months before the wedding, with an RSVP date of no later than 2 months before. That way, if you need to invite extra people, 2 months doesn't seem too last minute.

Obviously there is no rule that says you have to have a B or C list (remember, the fewer guests, the cheaper the wedding will be!) but in my experience most couples and their families end up with guest lists longer than they can realistically host, so it's a good way to compromise and keep everyone happy.

the
SETTING

HOW, WHEN, WHERE & WHY

SETTING
YOUR THEME

Once you've got a budget in mind, the next thing you need to decide is what you want the day to look and feel like, and when and where it will take place. Is your dream wedding big or small? Religious or not? Hosted in a nightclub, on a farm or in a pub? Which season is it happening in? Is there a special date you already have in mind? What colours, themes and styles are you initially drawn to?

I have been championing the idea of doing your wedding your way ever since the inception of Rock n Roll Bride. Even when I first started writing about weddings in 2007, it seemed mad to me that you wouldn't want your day to feel like a representation of you, your partner and the things you're obsessed with. In my view, the most enjoyable weddings are the ones that look and feel like an authentic expression of the couples' love and individuality. This is your party – your wedding, your rules!

I often hear couples post-wedding say 'Oh, we didn't really have a theme, we just wanted a day that felt like us'. So, instead of stressing yourself out trying to make everything match perfectly, you should embrace the organized chaos of your own imagination! That's what being an alternative bride is all about – bucking traditions that mean nothing to you, ignoring the things you don't care about and planning a wedding that feels authentic. What could be more joyful than a room filled with all your favourite people and all your favourite things?

When you first start looking through blogs, magazines and Pinterest, you will quickly grasp that when it comes to theming an alternative wedding, anything goes. The days of simply picking a signature colour and matching your bridesmaid dresses to the napkins and the flowers to the cake are long gone my friend! It's all about getting creative and bringing as much of yourself into your day as possible.

There is now an enormous range of venues and countless companies that will help you personalize every aspect of your day. In fact, there are so many options that narrowing your ideas down to a single style that works for you might feel like the biggest challenge. Don't let feeling initially overwhelmed get you down. This is an amazing opportunity for you to create your wedding exactly how you want it to be. Thinking of your day in terms of a concrete theme might feel very structured and restrictive, but in reality, it's just the framework on which you will base your decisions.

Think of your theme as something that will simply help unify the look of your wedding and make sure that the décor you create, the flowers you choose, the music you play and the clothes you both wear all feel like they fit together. If you're getting married in a tipi in a field, you are unlikely to want to wear a restrictive formal gown and 8-inch stilettos, I suspect you're actually the kind of bride who wants to rock a comfortable two-piece dress and her favourite biker boots.

Also, don't fret about the fact that your love of yoga will not 'go with' your partner's obsession with the *Back to the Future* franchise. They will work together because the two of you work together. Your differences are what make you awesome as a couple and they'll also be the things that make your wedding unique.

LOOK FOR INSPIRATION OUTSIDE OF THE WEDDING WORLD

Pinterest and wedding blogs are undoubtedly amazing for inspiration and ideas, but you also want your wedding to feel like YOU, not a carbon copy of someone else's day. Watch your favourite films, look at how companies you like brand themselves, go and visit the window displays of your favourite stores. You never know what might spark an idea, be it an unusual colour palette or a photo booth backdrop. Look in your closet and at how you've decorated your home. It's likely there will be a consistent dominant style and/or colours. Bring these things into your wedding too. Doing this will help you form a theme idea that feels unique, different and much more like the two of you.

WHAT DO YOU LOVE?

Both of you should write down all the things you really love – everything from your favourite bands to hobbies and fandoms. What are you obsessed with? What do you collect? What do you like to do with your spare time? Of course, you don't have to bring ALL these ideas into your wedding but it's a good way to get those ideas flowing.

There's no rule on how many things you should incorporate, but the less you have the simpler it will be when you come to actually choosing the items to include in your day.

It's also a good idea to choose a rough colour palette, and yes that can be 'all the colours' if you like! You'll want to have an overall guide though, for example earthy, natural tones won't necessarily sit well with a lot of black and white…If you're going for a rainbow scheme, decide on a bright rainbow or a pastel one. Keeping things consistent in hue and tone will make a more visually appealing event overall.

CREATE A MOOD BOARD

This might seem a little 'Type A' but even the most casual bride can benefit from a mood board. I'm sure I don't need to convince you that Pinterest is fantastic for collating your ideas, and to help you start to visualize how your day will look, but at some point, you might start to feel overwhelmed by all the options (for more on getting the most out of Pinterest, see page 78). Once you've been pinning away merrily for a while, you will start to notice recurring themes and the things and ideas you're most drawn to. Putting those favourites into a final mood board will help you drill down to what you really

want and clarify your ideas. It will also enable you to figure out what works together and what doesn't, AND they're a brilliant way for sharing your overall vision with suppliers/vendors too.

Once you've collated a lot of images that you like, print them all out (or if you're more technically minded, open them in Photoshop) and start pinning them to a large piece of paper or card. Seeing all these images together will help you to decipher the styles and colours that you naturally lean towards, and will highlight anything that doesn't fit in.

LESS IS MORE

If, like me, you have a penchant to go over the top and obsess about things, the 'less is more' rule can be hard to swallow, but eliminating things that don't fit the bigger picture is a really good idea. If you go OTT and incorporate too many competing ideas, the space could end up looking more like a hot mess than a wedding.

Picking a few key motifs is usually more visually effective than filling the room with STUFF.

Save your extra themes or ideas for the hen/bachelorette party, a big birthday party or even your future living room renovation! You don't have to throw everything at this one event.

CONSIDER THE VENUE

If you're getting married in a formal ballroom, those more outdoorsy, rustic details that you love might not really fit. Choosing a space that works with your theme, not against it, is vital for pulling off a cohesive event. Also, consider ways you can make use of any existing features in a space. Are there any large fireplaces that can be decorated, or impressive arches that you could have your ceremony under? Working with your venue, rather than against it, will always result in a more stylistically pleasing event and this is why I always advise choosing your venue before you start making any other big decisions.

CHOOSING YOUR VENUE

When it comes to planning your wedding, the venue is usually the first major decision you need to make. Not only is it often one of the biggest expenses, but most of your other subsequent choices will hinge on where the event is taking place.

The very first thing you need to decide is where you want to get married: will it be a local celebration, a destination wedding or are you planning to return to the place you grew up?

It's also worthwhile thinking about your guests' experience too. If everyone is local it will be pretty straight-forward, but if you're asking lots of people to travel there is more to consider. Is the venue in a convenient place for both drivers and those that need to get public transport? Does the venue offer accommodation or is there any nearby? Will it be affordable for everyone or will some people choose not to attend because it's too expensive? Will there be elderly guests who might not feel comfortable making a very long journey? Destination weddings may sound wonderful and romantic, but they can often be stressful and expensive for guests. If you want all your friends and family to be able to attend, then jetting off somewhere tropical might not be the best option. There's no right or wrong answer here – it all comes down to your priorities and who you want to be there.

After you've got your general location and the kind of venue you want decided, it's time to start looking for it. Answering the following questions before you begin will help you to narrow down the parameters of your search:

· What style of venue are you hoping for?
· How much do you want to spend?
· Do you want a package option (so the price also includes in-house catering, staff and/ or a co-ordinator) or do you want to organize everything yourselves?
· How many guests do you want to invite?
· Do you need any special provisions, such as disabled accessibility?
· Do you want to have your ceremony and reception in the same place?
· Do you want to invite children?
· Do you want to be able to supply your own alcohol?
· Would you prefer a 'blank canvas' to decorate yourselves or would you like somewhere already partly or fully decorated?

Finding a wedding venue is a bit like buying a house. I would always recommend taking the time to visit potential wedding venues in person. You don't want to disregard somewhere based on crappy photos online, because when you see it in real life it could be exactly what you are looking for! You also have to search for the potential in each place you see and think 'Will this work for us?' and/or 'Can we put our own stamp on it?' You should have your non-negotiables in mind but you may need to be a little more flexible in other aspects. If your ideas are unusual, your ideal venue in your dream location at your exact budget may not even exist!

What will you categorically not budge on? Maybe your dream is to have a woodland ceremony followed by live music, but you can't find a place that will allow you to have both. Are you willing to have the ceremony and reception in different places so you can achieve this? Would you be happy to compromise on the live music for the woodland ceremony? Are you able to widen your search location? If we've learned anything from watching endless hours of property TV shows, it should be that unless you have an unlimited budget, a reality check about what's available and what you can actually afford is needed from time to time.

PLANNING YOUR DÉCOR

It's a good idea to start planning your décor as soon as you have your venue booked, especially if you're going to be making a lot of it yourselves. Having a checklist (see right) is a great idea and means you'll be able to better plan out what needs making/designing/commissioning, and when.

ADVICE FOR DIY-ERS

I have to be honest with you here, I'm not the person to go to for DIY advice. I will hold my hands up and admit that I much prefer to outsource the things that I need made for an event to a professional or a much more talented friend. But we all know Rock n Roll brides are ALL about the homemade stuff so I will impart some of the DIY project advice I've gathered from working with brides over the years.

Start projects earlier than you think

Like, way earlier. DIY projects always take longer than you anticipate, so it's best to start them early to give yourself lots of time. The last thing you want is to be finishing off the centrepieces at 4am on the morning of your wedding!

Over-budget

Similarly, plan for things to end up costing more than you expect. There will always be additional costs that you'll have forgotten to account for.

Rope in helpers

Delegate, delegate, delegate! You do not have to make everything yourself, and your friends and family will probably be more than happy to be involved! Even the most particular of brides need to learn to let other people help them. It will be much more fun and wildly less stressful with an army of willing helpers. The hen/bachelorette party or bridal shower are really fun times to get crafting, or over Prosecco and cake on the weekends in the run up to the day.

Think about storage

Oh, you're planning to make a 6-foot octopus out of papier mâché to hang from the ceiling, are you? Great, where on earth are you going to store it? If you have a spare room or a garage, then prepare for them to be overrun with wedding stuff. If you don't have anywhere other than your immediate living areas, then think realistically about what you can put up with crowding your space and where things will live before (and after!) the wedding.

Learn when to let it go

Unless you are superhuman, it is likely that you won't have time to complete every single project idea that you've had. It sucks, but you just need to learn to let it go. Leave the least important projects until the end, so that if they don't get finished in time it doesn't matter as much.

DÉCOR CHECKLIST

This list of ideas is extensive and you don't need to include ALL these items, but it's a good jumping off point to start thinking about what you do and don't want at your wedding.

THE CEREMONY

- ☐ Welcome sign
- ☐ Information signs ('No photos please', 'Pick a seat, not a side' etc.)
- ☐ Aisle markers
- ☐ Aisle runners
- ☐ Reserved seat notices
- ☐ Ceremony arch
- ☐ Ceremony backdrop
- ☐ Ceremony items for table

THE TABLES

- ☐ Centrepieces
- ☐ Table runners
- ☐ Place cards
- ☐ Table names/numbers
- ☐ Menus
- ☐ Place mats

- ☐ Chargers
- ☐ Plates
- ☐ Cutlery
- ☐ Glasses
- ☐ Napkins
- ☐ Favours

RECEPTION SPACE

- ☐ Table plan
- ☐ Guest book
- ☐ Gift table
- ☐ Directional signs
- ☐ Cake/dessert table display
- ☐ Photo booth backdrop
- ☐ Lighting
- ☐ Hanging décor
- ☐ Miscellaneous props

DÉCOR *inspiration*

CENTREPIECES

The centrepieces on your tables are one of the easiest ways to add personality to your reception space. The possibilities are literally endless – the only limit is your imagination! See page 93 for a list of ideas to get you started.

PLACE SETTINGS

Most catering companies (or your venue) will be able to provide crockery, cutlery and linens. However, there's no reason why you have to use their standard options. You could collect vintage crockery from charity shops, car boot sales or eBay. Or how about using disposable and eco-friendly bamboo plates like the one above?

GUEST INFORMATION

There are certain things your guests need to know on the big day, such as the running order, where the bathrooms are, the dance floor rules (vitally important!) and where they're sitting. You will likely have various signs dotted around your venue so having them tie in with your overall theme will give a cohesive look.

GENERAL ROOM DÉCOR

To really add the wow factor, think about how you can incorporate extra decorations around the room – on the backs of chairs, hanging on the walls, dangling from the ceiling, on occasional tables or tucked in cosy corners. Adding décor beyond table centrepieces will really make a big impact and tie everything together.

your
STYLE

BEING YOUR MOST FABULOUS SELF

CHOOSING YOUR DRESS

For most brides, alternative or not, what they're going to wear on their wedding day is one of the first things they think about when they get engaged. I know I was browsing wedding dress websites at work the very next day!

When I got married in 2008, the choices were very limited. It was either A-line, princess or mermaid shaped; white, ivory or champagne in colour and always, *always* strapless. I mean, I'm sure more alternative gowns existed, but they were very hard to come by. Nowadays, you're much more likely to feel overwhelmed with all the options, colours and styles available!

There are designers who will literally make you any dress you can dream up, and even the more traditional bridal brands are realizing that brides these days want a much more diverse range of colours, fabrics and flattering shapes.

When it comes to finding your dream dress, you have the following seven main options:

HIGH STREET/OFF-THE-RACK

While some established clothing stores have stocked affordable 'off-the-rack' bridal dresses for a long time, in recent years, many more well-known high-street and online retailers have got wise to the demand, and added ranges of wedding dresses to their standard line up. This is a great option for brides on a budget who want to buy a dress quickly without any fuss.

Places to look
- ASOS
- Monsoon
- Phase 8
- Debenhams
- Coast
- BHLDN
- Whistles
- Needle and Thread
- Ted Baker
- Chi Chi London
- Collectif
- ModCloth
- Free People
- Missguided

PROS
- Typically cheaper than made-to-order
- Dresses are available right away
- You can try on many options in the comfort of your own home and return if they're no good

CONS
- Lower quality design and craftsmanship with probably less elaborate detailing
- You won't have the once-in-a-lifetime experience of the other options
- No customization or alternations available – you'd need to arrange these yourself
- New designs are usually only released in the spring and available for a limited time

MADE-TO-ORDER FROM A BRIDAL BOUTIQUE

This is how the majority of bridal boutiques operate. You try on sample dresses in store, then choose the one you want and they order for you from the designer in your (nearest) size. Between 6–8 months later, your dress will arrive at the boutique and you'll return for fittings.

Places to look
· Rock the Frock (Essex and Berkshire, UK)
· Mirror Mirror London (London, UK)
· Halo & Wren Bridal (Hertfordshire, UK)
· Morgan Davies (Hertfordshire and London, UK)
· The Case of the Curious Bride (Manchester, UK)
· David's Bridal (UK and USA)
· Shareen (New York and LA)

PROS
· Lots of choice all in one place
· Dresses can usually have small design customizations (such as adding or removing straps and shortening hemlines)
· The boutique will offer an in-house alternation and fittings service (for an extra fee)

CONS
· Sample sizes can be very limited, so you might be trying on dresses that are way too big or small for you and/or not in your preferred colour – so it can be hard to visualize how the dress will actually look
· You will need to order your dress a good 6–8 months before the wedding (as opposed to the ideal 4–6 months for most other options who can generally be more flexible)

DIRECT FROM THE DESIGNER'S SHOWROOM

If you have your heart set on a specific designer, most of them have their own bridal showrooms that you can visit. They will often offer more options when it comes to customization and you can see their entire range, rather than just the small selection that whichever bridal boutique you visited chose to carry.

Places to look
· Katya Katya London (London, UK)
· Lucy Can't Dance (Essex, UK)
· Legend Bridal Designs (Lancashire, UK)
· Otaduy (Barcelona, Madrid, Valencia)
· Ritual Unions (Berlin, Germany)
· Christian Siriano (New York, USA)
· Grace Loves Lace (London, LA, Gold Coast)
· House of Ollichon (London, UK)
· E&W Couture (Cardiff, UK)
· Bowen Dryden (Hertfordshire, UK)

PROS
· The designer themselves will be creating your gown
· You can see and try on their entire range
· Your dress will be made to your exact measurements rather than to the closest size and then altered to fit

CONS
· A designer will probably only have one location, which may or may not be convenient to get to for appointments and fittings

ONLINE DESIGNER

There are many bridal designers who don't have bricks-and-mortar stores, or choose to also sell their gowns online, direct to the customers. The process of working with a designer in this way will be similar to going direct to the designer but all the consultations will be done over the phone, Skype or email. You'll be responsible for measuring yourself too.

Places to look

- Chotronette
- Cleo & Clementine
- Honeypie Boutique
- Kitty & Dulcie
- Evey Clothing
- Sweet Caroline Styles

PROS

- You can buy from a designer that's not local to you, without ever having to leave the house!
- There are many talented creative designers out there, hence a lot of choice

CONS

- You can't try the dress on before you order
- You'll be responsible for your measurements being accurate
- The dress will be made for you so usually no returns will be offered
- Any additional alternations needed will be your responsibility
- If a designer is based in a different country to you, you may need to pay customs charges on shipping to receive your dress

BESPOKE/CUSTOM-MADE

Having a bespoke dress made for you is one of the most exciting and creative ways that you can choose your gown. You will work directly with a designer to pick everything from the shape and the fabric to the colour and the embellishments. If you can't find what you want from what's available elsewhere, this is a brilliant option.

Places to look

- The Couture Company (Birmingham, UK)
- Velvet Johnstone (London, UK)
- Beyond Bridal (London, UK)
- Rosie Red Corsetry (Oxfordshire, UK)

PROS

- Your dress can literally be ANYTHING you want it to be
- Unlimited choice and options
- Often perceived as the most expensive choice but that is not always the case if you have a budget to work to
- No one else will have a wedding dress the same as yours

CONS

- You have to use your imagination in the planning stages
- Unlimited choice can be overwhelming for some people!
- You won't be able to try it on until it's ready so you need to be sure the shape and the style are definitely what you want and will suit you

VINTAGE

Whether you want to wear a gown that's been in your family for generations or you just love the idea of picking up something in a retro style, choosing a vintage gown is a lovely way to incorporate a bygone era that you appreciate, whilst also expressing your own personal sense of style. There is something so romantic and magical about wearing a vintage wedding dress that already has its own history before you've worn it.

Places to look
- Etsy
- Elizabeth Avey Vintage
- The Vintage Wedding Dress Company
- Annie's Vintage Clothing
- Heavenly Vintage Brides
- Mill Crest Vintage

PROS
- It's unlikely that anyone else will have the same dress as you
- The dress can be altered to be brought up to date or to fit you perfectly
- Often a cheaper option

CONS
- There will only be one dress available and it might not be your size
- There could be some damage or discolouration that would need to be fixed
- They can be very delicate

SECOND-HAND

Many brides choose to sell their dresses after their wedding day in order to recoup some money or just to save it from languishing in the back of their closet. Be sure to find out if a second-hand dress has had any alterations before you buy it. If a bride has had their dress altered to fit them, even if it's listed at the size you want, it may not fit you in exactly the same way as ones you've previously tried on do.

Places to look
- Bridal Reloved
- Stillwhite
- Preloved
- Once Wed
- Preowned Wedding Dresses
- Oxfam Bridal
- Barnardos Bridal Rooms

PROS
- You could pick up a total bargain
- An environmentally conscious option
- Sometimes gowns haven't even been worn before – they're being sold because the bride has simply changed her mind

CONS
- If you are looking for a specific gown, it might be a long search to find it
- Dresses may need cleaning or extra alternations
- If you are buying direct from a bride, there will usually be no returns offered

ALTERNATIVE STYLE *inspiration*

THE BOHO BRIDE

Perfect for laid-back babes who'd
rather be running barefoot through their
festival-inspired wedding than wearing
fancy heels and an elaborate up-do!
Dresses are floaty and comfortable,
make-up is usually minimal and your hair
can be as wild and free as you are!
Dress: E&W Couture
Veil: Beyond Bridal

THE GOTHIC BRIDE

If black is your signature colour, then
there's no way you should be expected
to wear virginal white on your wedding
day. If you love embracing the darker
side of life, this should be how you
saunter down the aisle too!
Dress: Legends Bridal
Earrings: Rock n Rose

THE RETRO ROCKABILLY BRIDE

The perfect look for cute and quirky girls who love nothing more than a splash of colour. If you feel like you were born in the wrong era, then this modern take on a retro style will be your wedding dress dream come true!

Dress: The Couture Company
Shoes: Irregular Choice
Veil: Rock n Roll Bride x Crown and Glory

THE LAS VEGAS BRIDE

Have you always dreamed of dashing off to Vegas and eloping on your own terms? Nothing screams Sin City more than a dress adorned with sequins!
Dress: Chotronette
Hair clips: AM Faulkner

VEILS & HEADPIECES

Whether you think you want to wear one or not, I believe every bride should try on at least one veil. First of all, this is probably the only time in your life you'll have a legit reason to rock one, and secondly, nothing else has the power to completely transform your wedding day look. Whatever kind of dress you've picked, there's a veil that will work with it.

BIRDCAGE VEIL

Birdcage veils (*pictured above*) are short and made of netting. They sit just over the eyes and are a great option if you don't want the fuss of something longer. Adorable with a retro or vintage-inspired look.

BLUSHER VEIL

Blusher veils (*pictured left*) are usually made of tulle. They clip to the back of the head and sit on or just above the shoulders. Perfect if you don't want something over your face.

CIRCLE VEIL

Circle veils (*pictured left*) fall around midway down your upper arm. Cut in a circle with the fastening secured in the middle, a circle veil can be worn in front of the face, if required, or in a double layer behind the head. They look super cute with a tea-length or shorter dress.

FINGERTIP OR BALLET VEIL

Fingertip or ballet veils (*pictured below*) are usually around 1 m/3 ft long. They should fall somewhere around your fingertips when your arms are at your sides, though there will be some natural variation depending on your height. A really versatile option, these work well with both long and short dresses.

CATHEDRAL VEIL

Cathedral veils (*pictured above*) are the longest veil option, around 3 m/10 ft. They will trail beyond even the most elaborate dress, and are perfect for a bride who really wants to make a statement! Chapel or church length veils give a similar striking effect but with a slightly shorter train of around 2 m/6$\frac{1}{2}$ ft.

HEADPIECE *inspiration*

MERMAID SHELL TIARA

This look is perfect for brides who want to unleash their inner mermaid! An alternative twist on the traditional tiara, they're usually made from shells, pearls and other beach-inspired motifs.
Tiara pictured: Rachel Luna Webb
Also check out: Chelsea's Flower Crowns and Aurora Moon Headwear

BRIGHT FLOWER CROWN

A bright flower crown can be made from the same blooms as your bouquet to tie your look together, or you could pick out the colours from your shoes or bridesmaid dresses. They're ideal for a laid-back but fun-loving festival bride.
Crown pictured: Crown and Glory
Also check out: Rock N Rose and Gypsy Rose Vintage

CELESTIAL HALO CROWN

Stars are a favourite detail for Rock 'n' Roll brides, and hair accessories are an easy way to add celestial vibes to your day. This crown can also be worn to adorn the back of the head – perfect if your dress is all party at the front!
Crown pictured: Crown and Glory
Also check out: Tilly Thomas Lux and Erica Elizabeth Designs

MODERN SEQUIN HEADBAND

This super fun holographic sequin headband is a modern twist on the traditional Alice band hair accessory. It would look fantastic with a 60s-style mini dresses or a relaxed two-piece gown. Great for an urban city ceremony or for running around Vegas!
Headband pictured: AM Faulkner
Also check out: Lizzie McQuade and Beretkah

SURVIVING THE BRIDAL BOUTIQUE EXPERIENCE

On wedding TV shows and in the movies, dress shopping always goes a little bit like this: the bride and a gaggle of girlfriends go to a fancy boutique where everyone drinks Champagne while she tries on dress after dress until one makes her cry because it is The One. However, the reality is usually very different.

First of all, most boutiques do not give away free Champagne and many of them limit the number of people you can bring with you. It will likely be just you and one or two allies, and you may also be limited as to the number of gowns you can try on per appointment.

Like with everything in the wedding industry, there are some truly phenomenal bridal boutiques, who will go out of their way to make you feel comfortable and will provide the most wonderful service whatever your body shape, budget or priorities, and there are others who, in short, will not.

For some, the whole experience can be quite the ordeal. I've heard it all – subtle (or not so subtle) body shaming, eye rolls about meagre budgets and stories about salespeople being pushy or condescending. But it doesn't have to go down like that.

Call ahead

If you have particular concerns, such as sizing or your budget, pick up the phone and speak to somebody before you book an appointment. Not everyone will be able to help you, some may be downright rude, but at least you'll have saved yourself the hassle of a visit if they're not the boutique for you. You want to find somewhere where the salespeople are informed, confident, and excited to be working with you. If you don't get that by speaking to them on the phone, then keep looking until you find somewhere that is.

Make an appointment

While there's nothing wrong with popping into a bridal shop just to see what they have, it's unlikely that you'll be able to try anything on without an appointment. Bridal boutiques get especially busy at weekends, so if you are able to make an appointment for a weekday, then you might be given more time as they won't be rushing you out to fit all the appointments in.

Arrive in plenty of time

Being punctual is really important. Your appointment will likely be limited to a fixed amount of time, so if you're late you'll only be eating into your allotted time.

Limit the number of people you bring

It's a good idea to bring someone with you for moral support and to give their opinion, but don't bring everyone you know. Having too many opinions will probably only confuse you. We've all seen *Say Yes to the Dress* TV episodes where the bride loves a gown but as soon as she shows it to the 15 family members she's brought with her and someone says they don't like it, she changes her mind. Whoever you bring, make sure it's someone who understands your style and whose opinion you trust.

Be open to suggestions from salespeople

Even if you're very specific about what you do or do not want, listen to your salesperson's advice. While you should be clear from the outset about your non-negotiables (there's no point in trying on a dress that you absolutely hate), do be open to trying on new colours, shapes and styles that you might not have considered before. You may be surprised about what you end up liking when you put it on. Wedding dresses have this canny knack of looking completely different on an actual human body than they do on the hanger.

Wear good underwear

Nude knickers and a well-fitting strapless bra are a must. They'll make the dresses look their best, but also the sales assistant may need to help you into a gown, so this is probably not the time for a hot pink thong or going commando.

Ask if you can take photos

This is a highly contentious issue and some bridal boutiques will refuse to let you take photos, whereas others will actively encourage it. Just make sure you check before you whip the camera out. If you are allowed, I'd definitely recommend it. Being able to go away, sleep on it and consider how the dress looked on you in the cold light of day is very helpful. It's easy to rush into choosing a dress with all the excitement of an appointment (or just because you want the ordeal to be over!) and then regret it later. Don't be afraid to take a few days to consider everything before you place your order.

No body shaming allowed!

We've all heard horror stories of salespeople who ask you if you're going to lose weight, or who body shame you generally with thoughtless comments. This is not 'just how it is', those are shitty salespeople who do not deserve your money. If someone tries to shame you, or makes you feel uncomfortable about your size, feel free to tell them (nicely) that it's none of their business and to either leave or ask for someone different to help you.

There are other options

When it comes to dress shopping brides tend to fall into two camps: those who love everything about the experience and others who would rather shove hot pokers through their eyeballs. If you find the idea of visiting a bridal boutique for your wedding gown too much, THEN YOU DO NOT HAVE TO. These days there are so many alternative options (see pages 44-48), so whatever your priorities are, you can find something that you feel your most fabulous self in, in the least stressful way for you.

HAIR & MAKE-UP

Whether you're booking a professional or going down the DIY route, the key to looking and feeling your best is choosing a hairstyle and make-up look that feels like you. Bridal style does not have to be boring, it doesn't have to be classic or elegant and it certainly does not have to be natural (unless that's what YOU want!).

THE BEST HAIR OF YOUR LIFE

In order for your hair to look its absolute best on your wedding day, start taking proper care of it now. Especially if your locks are a bit damaged, invest in some salon-quality products, get regular cuts, and if you're planning on a big colour change, then you'll want to begin that process as early as possible too.

I've been dyeing my hair various different colours of the rainbow since I was 16 years old. It's gone through stages of being so brittle that it broke off every time I brushed it, to stretchy and stringy when wet. However, over the past five years or so, it's been my mission to keep my hair colourful AND healthy, and although it takes a bit of time and money, it's never looked better.

If your hair snaps off or won't grow past a certain length, then it is likely lacking in MOISTURE, so I would recommend starting to use a moisture-rich shampoo, conditioner and treatments. I love the Moroccan Oil brand, Redken's 'All Soft' range and Pureology Perfect 4 Platinum shampoo and conditioner.

If your hair is stretchy and stringy when wet, then it's probably lacking PROTEIN. Hair is made up of protein and if it gets damaged by heat or chemicals (such as bleach), then it will degrade the proteins that make up the outer layer, exposing the cortex. Protein-rich products such as Redken's 'Extreme' range will help restore it, patch up the frayed cortex and smooth the outer layer. It's important that you only use protein-rich products while your hair is still at the stringy-when-wet stage, otherwise you could end up with a build-up that can make your hair snap with very little effort. Once your hair has recovered from the stringy stage, mix it up with a more moisture-intensive product and only use the protein-rich ones every few weeks.

Olaplex is a revolutionary product which protects hair while it's being bleached. When Olaplex is added to the bleach, it not only protects your locks from being further damaged by the process, but it also repairs the already broken disulfide bonds (which are what give hair its elasticity and strength). Olaplex is a three-stage process: Steps 1 and 2 are done at the salon and you can buy step 3 to take home and use once a week to keep your hair healthy!

I have also been taking fish oil supplements every day for the past few years. My favourite is Xtendlife Omega 3 DHA Fish Oil (available online). As well as helping keep your heart, joints and brain healthy, Omega 3 helps prevent hair breakage and encourages new hair growth.

Clip-in hair extensions are a great affordable option if you want to add temporary lustrous length for your wedding. If your hair is a fantasy colour (blue, green, pink etc.), buy the lightest blonde real hair ones you can find and simply dye them to match. Among other places, they are available from Sally Beauty professional hair and beauty stores and from Amazon.

HAIRDRESSERS I LOVE
· Lovehair Co. (UK)
· Elbie van Eeden (UK)
· Le Keux Vintage Salon (UK)
· Lipstick & Curls (UK)
· Kristen Jackson (New York)
· Hair by Kasey (LA)

MAKE-UP MASTERCLASS

When it comes to wedding make-up, you want to consider three main things:
1. Wearing something that will last all day
2. Making sure it will photograph well
3. Choosing a look that you feel your most gorgeous, confident self in

Skin first

The real key to make-up that looks its best and lasts all day is providing it with a great base to start with, and that means skincare! If you haven't had a skincare routine before, now is the time to start. You don't need to spend a lot of money either. Using a good cleanser morning and night, followed by a toner and moisturizer suitable for your skin type will make the world of difference. I like to use a toner with glycolic acid, which minimizes pores and improves my skin texture overall.

I personally love The Ordinary's skincare range. Stripping back unnecessary packaging and misleading ingredients lists, they offer an abundance of brilliant products at reasonable prices. The Glossier brand is another one of my skincare favourites.

Ensuring your make-up lasts all day

After years of trial and error I've found that, for me, the secrets to making my make-up last all day are using a primer, investing in a good foundation and concealer (it's true that the more expensive brands tend to be better) and applying them with a damp Beautyblender sponge. I fix it with a dusting of translucent powder, which I go over with my Beautyblender again. I finish off with a truck-load of fixing spray (Urban Decay's All Nighter is my go-to). However, everybody's skin is different so, especially if you're doing your make-up yourself, you will want to experiment with various techniques and products. YouTube is fantastic for make-up tutorials, product recommendations and advice.

Sunscreen

If you want to keep your skin looking its best you should be wearing a sunscreen, or use make-up with an in-built sunscreen, every day. A lot of brides worry that wearing sunscreen will create a 'white cast' over their face in the photos, but unless your photographer is using direct flash, this won't be the case. If you are having a winter wedding or your venue is very dark, you might want to skip wearing it on the wedding day.

Practice makes perfect

If you're doing your own wedding day make-up then practice, practice, practice. Wear it all day to see how it lasts, try it out in different lights, and importantly, see how it photographs. It's important that your foundation matches your skin-tone, so if you are planning on getting a spray tan for the wedding be sure to do a trial run of that too and buy foundation to match!

If you have booked a professional make-up artist, then ask if you can do a trial. You want to check that you're on the same page stylistically and that you like what they do. Not all make-up artists are created equal!

MAKE-UP ARTISTS I LOVE

· Louise Seymour (UK)
· Alison Cameron (UK)
· Joyce Connor (UK)
· Nicola Honey (UK)
· Your Beauty Call (Las Vegas)
· Regan Rabanal (New York)

HAIR *inspiration*

LIGHT IT UP

It's important to have fun with your hair and here we went with a 'more is more' approach. We entwined battery-powered fairy lights into this mega-braid, but you could also use them in a cute chignon or to light up a simpler style. They look stunning in darker hair, but please remember to check that your lights are safe before trying this look.

FLOWER CHILD

This is essentially two Dutch braids secured in bunches at the base of the neck, but what gives it life is the addition of the flowers! We chose bright, fluffy flowers to contrast with the model's glossy black hair, but chat to your florist and/or hairstylist about what would work for you. Flowers can also be wired to help them last longer.

COOL-GIRL WAVES

This is a great option for long or short hair and with or without volume. Our model's edgy purple bob was cool enough, so we kept it simple with a side parting and curled hair in opposite directions to create waves with a bit of movement.

TOP KNOT

After adding waves to the hair (*as left*), take a section on top of the head from the hair line to the crown. Find the highest point of the brow, as this is a good natural place to start your section so that it's not too wide. Pull this into a small hair band at the crown, in a half-up style, then gently backcomb and twist into a mini bun. Secure with hair grips/ bobby pins and finish with hair spray.

MAKE-UP *inspiration*

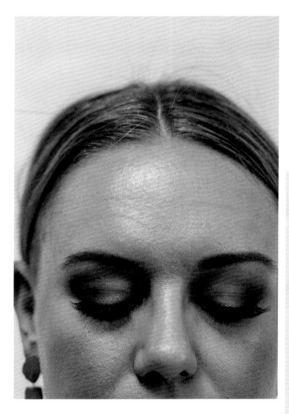

EXAGGERATED EYES

A classic black winged eyeliner is a staple for many brides on their wedding day, but why not give it some Amy Winehouse vibes and elongate and over-exaggerate the flick? This is a gorgeous, yet easy to pull off look. *Pictured: Tattoo Liner in 'Trooper' by Kat Von D.*

RAINBOW MAGIC

If you want a fun pop of ALL THE COLOURS then a striking rainbow eye is a really cool idea. If you're looking to create this yourself, make sure you invest in some highly pigmented make-up so it's as bright as possible! *Pictured: Ultimate Shadow Palette in Bright by NYX.*

PINK POP

Your eyeliner doesn't have to be black! This pop of pink is ideal for brides who love colour. *Pictured: Chromaline in Process Magenta by MAC.*

METALLIC MAIDEN

Add an edgy twist to a classic red lip with a sweep of glitter, either on your lids or under the eyes. This look is perfect for the bride who loves to sparkle. *Pictured: Coarse Multi Gel Glitter in Silver by Kryolan.*

DRESSING YOUR BRIDESMAIDS

Finding a dress for yourself can be stressful enough without also having to deal with the overwhelming task of getting one perfect outfit that all your best friends will want to wear as well. How can you make five women, who all have different body shapes and tastes, happy all at the same time? How can you be chill about the whole thing while also getting the vision that you want? If you have boys on your side of the wedding party, how can you make sure they feel, and look, included and not like groomsmen? How do you avoid turning bridesmaid dress shopping into a full-time job?

Needless to say, it can be an extremely daunting and time-consuming experience. Unless your babes are all super-chilled and happy to wear whatever you give them, you'll need a plan of attack.

LET THEM MAKE THE DECISION

This might go against everything any other wedding book or magazine has ever told you, but unless you are really, REALLY specific about what you want your bridesmaids to wear, it will be much less stressful if you let them make the final decision.

The likelihood is that they'll know what shapes and styles suit them and the good news is that a mismatched approach can look just as fantastic (in some cases even more so) than everyone rocking exactly the same frock.

GIVE THEM SOME GUIDELINES

If you're going for this approach, then the key to making it work is to have at least one element that ties all the outfits together. That can be the colour, the shape, the fabric or even just having them in the same accessories.

Tell your bridesmaids that they can wear whatever they like as long as it's a pale grey maxi/brightly coloured short dress with a 50s silhouette/gold sequined dress, and then let them each pick something themselves.

MIX 'N' MATCH

Another approach is to put each person in the same shaped dress but in a different colour. The rainbow or ombré effect looks really fantastic in photos and gives each bridesmaid the option of picking a colour that suits them.

INCLUDE THE BOYS

If you're having 'bridesmen' as part of your side of the wedding party, then the same rules apply. Pick a part of the boys' outfits to tie in with the bridesmaids rather than the groomsmen, whether that be with accessories such as a bow tie and pocket square in the same fabric, shirts that match the colour of the dresses or even entire suits made to match.

BUY SEASONALLY

There are many companies who specialize in bridesmaid dresses. Check out Maid to Measure, For Her and For Him, BHLDN and ModCloth for some great options. However, if you want to save money on your bridesmaid outfits, then the high street/shopping mall is your best bet.

Be sure to think seasonally with your shopping though. Autumn/fall colours such as burgundy, mustard, burnt orange or dark green will likely only really be available to buy from September onwards, whereas if you're going for a pastel colour scheme, this will be much easier to find in the spring.

SPEAK YOUR MIND

It's very easy to get caught up in trying to keep everyone else happy when you're planning a wedding. That probably just means you're a very good friend, but you don't want what's really important to you to get lost in the crowd. I find that the best approach when dealing with lots of people's opinions is to communicate clearly what you want as early as possible. If you really don't give two hoots about what your bridesmaids wear, then awesome, but it is a good idea to give them *some* sort of guidelines, or they may end up looking more like guests than part of the wedding party.

LET'S HEAR IT FOR THE BOYS

It's a curious phenomenon in the wedding industry that although many of the traditions have quite patriarchal undertones, when it comes to the details of planning the day, men are kind of ignored. It's almost as if the wedding industry doesn't think they'll be interested in the organization of their own wedding at all. Everything is firmly centred around The Bride. Obviously, this is a pretty stereotypical view and let's not even consider what this means for men in same-sex relationships.

This probably stems from the fact that women, historically, simply had more time to devote to wedding planning, as men were the main bread-winners in the home. Nowadays, it is more likely that both sexes have similar amounts of time to devote to planning their day. Secondly, there's a lot less pressure on men to stick to the old-fashioned reserved masculinity stereotype, they now feel more comfortable displaying their own creativity, passions and emotions alongside women.

In my experience, men are now just as interested in wedding planning as women. It's simply the outdated wedding industry view that assumes that they aren't. Because of this, frustratingly, the 'wedding ready' outfit options for men, beyond the obvious and traditional, are quite limited. However, if you're willing to put some effort in and think outside the box a little bit, guys can easily find something unique and fabulous to wear too!

HIRE

There are thousands of places that rent out suits such as Moss Bros, Slaters and Men's Wearhouse, to name a few. The reason for going down this route usually comes down to budget – it's certainly one of the more affordable and convenient options too, as there are chains for these stores all over the place. It's a particularly good idea for groomsmen, as each one can visit the branch they are closest to, be fitted, collect and return the suit themselves.

PROS
· Affordable
· Readily available
· Lots of options (though nothing too out there!)

CONS
· The fit might not be brilliant
· No alterations
· You don't get to keep it afterwards

HIGH STREET/SHOPPING MALL

There are countless shops that sell suits. I don't think I really need to list them all here, but the great thing about going for the high street option is simply that – ALL THE OPTIONS. Somewhere that does affordable, but slightly more unique suit options is ASOS. The best part of buying from them is you can order loads to try on at home and then return the ones that are no good. You can also usually buy each piece individually. This means that if you're not a standard size, or you'd prefer to go for a mix 'n' match look, you can do so easily.

PROS
· Loads of choice
· Try on in your own time and return if no good
· Mix 'n' match your favourite pieces to create your own look

CONS
· You might not end up with the most unique outfit
· Any additional tailoring will be down to you
· Some of the choice will be dictated by trends/ seasons

CUSTOM MADE

If you have a bigger budget (expect to pay upwards of £1000/$1200), then having a suit custom made is a fantastic option. Not only will you get something one-of-a-kind and made to your exact taste but it will also fit you like a glove. Check out Jack Bunneys, Cad & The Dandy and A Suit That Fits or find a local tailor who offers a bespoke service.

PROS
· Unlimited choice of colours, fabrics and styles
· No one else will have a suit the same as yours
· Excellent craftsmanship
· An opportunity to invest in a suit you feel truly comfortable in, that you can keep forever

CONS
· All the options can be overwhelming if you don't know what you really want
· Usually one of the most expensive options

FINDING YOUR STYLE

Morning suits, evening suits, three-piece suits, casual suits, tuxedos… When it comes to the style of what you wear, the choice really is yours. The most popular option for a British wedding is still the morning suit, but if that's too boring or traditional for you, there are plenty of other ways to go about it!

THINK ABOUT THE SEASON & THE THEME

Look at your wedding theme and think about what will suit it. If you're having a laid-back beach or high-summer wedding, then a more casual suit in a light colour and soft fabric

(linen, cotton or light wool) would look and feel great. If you're having a mid-winter wedding, then you might want to rock some jewel tones such as deep burgundy or bring out some velvet, wool or tweed. And if you're having an epic *Lord of the Rings* themed day, well this is your chance to dress up like Legolas if you want to!

You don't have to go for obvious black, blue or grey either. A colourful or patterned suit makes an amazing impression. If you are going for a bold colour, then a fabric with a matt appearance (rather than shiny) will absorb light rather than reflect it. This will make the colour appear richer and look better in photographs.

GO YOUR OWN WAY

You want to feel comfortable and like yourself, so if you're not a formal suit kinda guy, then it isn't the only option. Honestly, if you want to rock up in jeans and trainers (maybe buy some smart new ones though), then do it! A slightly less scruffy, but still casual, approach could be chinos or smart casual trousers, a long-sleeved patterned shirt with an open collar and a blazer. For a more indie look, swap out a tie or cravat for a patterned or colourful bow tie.

If you're really into thrifting or buying second-hand, then this is where you should start the search for your wedding outfit too.

Check out Tweed Addict for loads of awesome tweed options and The Vintage Suit Hire Company if your style is inspired by the past.

FINISHING TOUCHES

Think about the wedding theme, but also collaborate with the bridal party to decide how your accessories can complement what they are wearing and vice versa. Matching a tie, bow tie, braces or pocket square to their colours is a great way to bring your looks together. Choosing similar buttonholes and bouquets looks really effective too.

the FUN STUFF

PERSONALIZING YOUR DAY

IT'S TIME TO GET CREATIVE!

Here's when things really start to get fun, it's time to craft your heart out (or, if the idea of that makes you want to cry, to book some suppliers to make your creative vision a reality!).

Personalizing your day is all about bringing the things you love in everyday life into your wedding. If you love travelling, how about having a vintage map as the table plan? If you love nothing more than curling up with your favourite romantic novel, how about using them as part of your centrepieces? If you're really into comics, why not use your favourites as the table names and markers? Obsessed with tattoos? Have a temporary tattoo station. Big foodies? Theme the day around your favourite grub… you get the idea. Once you get started, the ideas will just start flowing and you won't be able to stop!

A WORD ABOUT PINTEREST

Pinterest is awesome but it can also be a bit of an evil temptress, distracting you from your original vision and offering you lots of shiny new options. It's great for the initial gathering of ideas, searching for DIY projects and collecting your inspiration all in one place, but sooner or later it might start to feel overwhelming. You know full well you're having a comic book theme with bright pops of colour, but oooh, look sequins… a Disney-inspired wedding cake… a floaty bohemian dress… pretty! If you let it, Pinterest can not only take over your life, it can completely divert you from what you wanted your wedding to look like in the first place.

Here's how to get the best out of Pinterest and show it who's boss. Start with a general wedding board. Pin anything and everything you like. This part is really fun! After a while you'll start to notice recurring themes and ideas, you might even be able to see what's working together and what definitely is not. When you're ready to commit, start a whole new board and move over only the pins that fit the theme you've decided on.

After a while, come back to your new board, glance over it and observe any common colours, themes and ideas. Delete any that are obviously jarring or just don't fit. It's now time to be realistic too. Ask yourself, is this something you could feasibly include in your day or do you just really like it? Delete anything that won't work with your theme, venue or location. There's no point pinning lots of beautiful images of sunny desert elopements if you're getting married in Manchester in November.

There are so many ideas and SO MANY THINGS you could do, but this is only one wedding! You can only include a certain number of ideas. As I've mentioned already, you do not need to throw every idea or theme you've ever loved at this one event. You can always save them for a birthday party, your hen/bachelorette party or another special occasion.

STATIONERY & PAPER GOODS

Save the Date cards, invitations, the order of service, menus, place cards, general signage… All of these things come under your wedding stationery. The paper goods can be as big, or as small, a part of your day as you wish. If you're the kind of person who loves snail mail, who sends their besties cards in the post at any given opportunity, then the likelihood is that the paper goods are going to play a large part in the style and theme of your wedding. However, if you're perfectly happy to set up a Facebook group or email out your invites and call it a day, then you do 'you'!

SAVE THE DATE CARDS

The purpose of a Save the Date card is to, well… encourage your guests to do exactly that. You'd usually send these out as soon as you've got your date and venue sorted. It's kind of a 'Hey, we're getting married and we're definitely going to invite you, but not for a little while yet, but keep this date free, k?' message. They are certainly not compulsory and you don't have to send them if you don't want to, but they're a good idea if you are worried your key guests might get invited to another wedding, book a holiday or may need to arrange time off work to attend. If you have your theme pinned down in time, you can tie your Save the Date cards in with the same or similar design as your formal invitations.

FORMAL INVITATIONS

As well as letting your guests know when and where the wedding is happening, your formal invitations allow you to set the tone of your day beforehand and give your guests a sneak preview of what's in store. This is also usually your first chance to get really creative.

If you're having an outdoorsy festival-inspired day, you could have invites that look like a music festival line up or gig tickets. For a brightly coloured same-sex wedding, why not cover your invites in rainbows? For a sleek and modern city celebration, opt for something monochromatic and timelessly classic.

Whether you chose to make them yourself, or hire a stationer to do them for you, the essential information you need to include is:

· Your names
· Your parents' names (if they are hosting)
· The date and time
· The venue and general location
· RSVP information
· RSVP deadline

CHECK OUT

Wedfest (*pictured top right*)

Papier (*pictured below right*)

Sailor and Scout (*pictured page 83, above*)

Veronica Dearly (*pictured page 83, below*)

Lucy Ledger

Knots and Kisses

ADDITIONAL INFORMATION CARD

This is a great item to include with your formal invites, especially if your wedding is taking an unusual or alternative approach. This is the place where you can preemptively answer all those questions your guests might have.

THINGS TO INCLUDE

- Venue address, directions and parking information
- Accommodation options
- Gift list/gift registry information
- Menu options
- Itinerary of the day
- Whether children are invited
- Any dress code

You can also choose to set up a wedding website which will host all this information, but personally I think that something physical for your guests to hold in their hands, stick up on their refrigerator and refer back to will be much more useful to most people. I've received many invitations in the past that say 'Find more information on our wedding website', and only on one occasion have I actually bothered to go and check it out (eek, sorry!). While a wedding website allows you to add all sorts of bonus things like how you met and who the bridal party are, in all honesty your guests don't really need to know that stuff. What they need to know is if they have to bring cash for the bar and if their Sat Nav/GPS will take them to the venue easily or if they'll get lost down a wayward country lane.

ORDER OF SERVICE

The order of service specifically relates to your ceremony and gives your guests something to follow along with, so they know what's happening in what order. Some people like to include the complete breakdown of the service – including the words of the officiant and responses of the couple, whereas others use it only as a guide with the basic outline and maybe the words to the hymns or songs.

You can either leave these on seats or have the groomsmen hand them to each guest as they arrive. It's a nice idea if they're printed in the same style and colour scheme as your invitations so everything ties together.

THINGS TO INCLUDE

Front page
- Name of venue and location
- Your names
- The date and time

Inside
- The processional song
- Any hymns or song words
- The readings – title, author and 'read by…'
- The marriage ceremony
- The signing of the register
- The blessing
- Recessional song

You could also include an introduction to the wedding party, some words or a poem you've written for each other, or use it as your opportunity to thank the people who are involved (the person conducting the ceremony, the musicians or your parents).

MENU, PLACE CARDS, SIGNS, TABLE PLAN

The paper goods you include on your wedding day are one of the easiest ways to keep your theme going. They bring a personal touch to any venue and tie different elements of the day together, from the ceremony to the after-party. They also highlight any important information your guests might need to know, such as where they're sitting, what they're eating and what's happening when. The information to include on each of these items is pretty self-explanatory really. How simple or elaborate the designs are is completely up to you. Refer back to the décor checklist (page 39) for a more extensive list of items you might want to have made.

THANK-YOU CARDS

Again, these are pretty self-explanatory, but a really nice thing to do. Many couples include a photo from the wedding on the front too, which is a lovely touch. You should send a thank-you card to everyone who gave you a gift.

CATERING

Whatever kind of wedding you have, the food and drink are in prime position to make or break the day. Not only is it usually one of the biggest costs, but weddings are long days and good food will keep your guests happy and ready to party long into the evening!

Here are a few things you need to consider when making decisions about what kind of food and drink to serve.

WHAT DO YOU LIKE TO EAT?

The traditional sit-down three-course banquet is certainly not your only option and there are now more catering companies than ever offering delicious alternatives. Everything from afternoon tea to regional cuisine, gourmet BBQs/cookouts, burrito bars and wood-fired pizzas served from outdoor ovens! Food carts and trucks are also really popular. How about having a fish 'n' chip or taco truck arriving to feed your guests? Or serve them ice cream from a van for dessert? In lieu of a wedding cake, you could have a stack of donuts, a candy floss/ cotton candy vendor or a crêpe station!

Obviously, you want everyone to enjoy the food, but the world really is your delicious oyster when choosing it, so ultimately you should just pick the things you really love to eat!

DIETARY REQUIREMENTS

If you're a committed vegan or vegetarian, only serving food that suits your lifestyle choice is easier than ever. There are so many fantastic catering companies offering a wide range of delicious options. If it's something that defines you, or you feel passionate about, then of course you should reflect this in the food you serve at your wedding. Don't feel like you have to serve meat to please everybody else.

Giving plenty of options and offering a variety of dishes is a thoughtful way to serve a fully vegetarian or vegan menu to meat-eating guests. That way there are lots of dishes for people to try and if someone doesn't like something, then there will be other things for them to sample. Don't let them think that they'll be left starving because they're eating vegan food.

Remember to ask your guests if they have any dietary requirements or food allergies so that you can ensure the caterer you hire can accommodate them.

THINK SEASONALLY

Just like with flowers, food that's in season will be more delicious, fresh and affordable than anything that has to be shipped in overseas. Consider sourcing your ingredients locally if you'd like to support growers and producers in your area. Farmers' markets and independent restaurants are a great place to start.

FEEDING YOUR SUPPLIERS

Some of your wedding suppliers/vendors, particularly those who are there all day like photographers, will also need to be fed. Make sure you check your contracts and if you're not sure, ask them if they expect a meal. Most won't require a full three-course spread but some fries and a nice sandwich will be much appreciated! Most catering companies will offer a vendor meal option which is cheaper as well.

ALCOHOL

How you organize the drinks will most likely depend on your venue and budget. Your venue may have a cash bar but if you don't want to ask your guests to buy their own drinks, you'll need to buy these beforehand or put a certain amount behind the bar. Your venue may also offer a 'sale or return' option, meaning if something doesn't get opened they won't charge you for it. If you're planning to buy the drinks elsewhere and bring them in, remember to ask your venue about any corkage fees. The costs can be quite high and may make or break your DIY idea entirely.

At minimum you should provide a welcome drink and enough wine on the tables for each guest to have around half a bottle with their meal. The welcome drink can be as fancy as Champagne or a signature cocktail, but it can actually be anything you want – cans of beer in buckets for people to help themselves to, a 'Pimp your Prosecco' station or pitchers of Pimm's. Always offer an alcohol-free option as well.

THE CAKE

For some, the cake is the crowning glory of any wedding, and for others it's just an overpriced centrepiece that no-one really wants to eat.

If the cost is your main issue, think about serving the cake as your dessert rather than having it as an additional offering – most of your guests won't want both anyway!

Traditional three- or four-tiered wedding cakes can be very expensive (and honestly most people don't even like fruit cake and marzipan), so if you'd rather have something a bit more 'you', you're in luck because there are now so many great alternative options. See pages 86-87 for inspiration!

CAKE inspiration

PILE 'EM HIGH

If a tiered cake isn't your thing, think about what else you could serve instead. A tower of cupcakes was the first really novel innovation to sweep the wedding cake table, followed by more twists such as macarons, meringues, pies, cheese wheels and donuts! *Pictured below: Cake topper by Rachel Emma Studio.*

GET NAKED

'Naked' cakes fit well with a more rustic, country-vibes themed wedding. They can either be completely nude (just the sponge cake with no icing/frosting at all) or covered in a thin layer of frosting, or sprinkled with icing/confectioners' sugar for a 'semi-naked' look. Either way, a naked cake provides a nice neutral base for you to add your own personal style to with the decorations you choose – from fruits and edible flowers to shards of chocolate or, of course, a cute custom cake topper. *Pictured above: Cake by Blossom and Crumb.*

DESSERT TABLE DARLING

If you just can't settle on one cake, or you want to give your guests lots of things to choose from, then a dessert table will be right up your street! You could easily put this together yourself with store-bought or homemade treats, but there are also some creative companies who make utterly breathtaking themed dessert table spreads. *Pictured below: Desserts and cake by Gaya's Cakes.*

GET CREATIVE

If TV shows like *Extreme Cake Makers*, *Cake Boss* and *Amazing Wedding Cakes* have taught us anything, it's that the sky's the limit when it comes to creative artistry in wedding cakes. If you can dream it, you can probably find someone who will make it a sugarpaste or chocolatey reality for you! *Pictured above: Cake by the Tattooed Bakers.*

BOUQUETS

No matter how alternative you are, most brides (and bridesmaids) still want to carry a bouquet. They give nervous hands something to do and, let's face it, look great in the photos. But that doesn't mean real flowers are your only option, and actually, going for something else can often be cheaper. It also means you'll be able to keep it forever as a memento of the day.

PAPER FLOWERS

Making flowers out of paper opens up a lot of creative avenues, as you can use different kinds of paper to change up the entire look. Sheet music, comic books, thin card, pearly, shiny or metallic paper – there are so many things you can make paper blooms from. *Pictured above: Bouquet by May Contain Glitter.*

BUTTON OR BROOCH BOUQUETS

This is one of the most popular alternative options because you can get really creative with the design. Pick a colour or a strong theme and run with it! You could have a Barbie pink bouquet, one using every colour of the rainbow, something steampunk-inspired with cogs and wheels or a really gothic bouquet with black buttons and lots of skulls – the possibilities are practically endless! *Pictured above: Bouquet by Beaubuttons.*

SILK FLOWERS

Bouquets made of faux flowers are gaining popularity, particularly as the quality of the silk flowers has come on a long way in recent years. This could be an easy DIY option and places like HomeSense, TK Maxx and Hobby Craft (Home Goods, TJ Maxx and Michael's in the US) sell a good variety of them but there are also some fantastic companies making utterly stunning arrangements. *Pictured left: Bouquet by Crown and Glory.*

UNUSUAL BLOOMS

If you like real flowers, but want something unique for your bouquet, then fret not as there is plenty to choose from. Succulents, air plants, rainbow roses, banksias, protea, gingers, delphiniums, anthuriums, eremurus, leucodendrons and orchids are all beautiful choices. Be sure to ask your florist's advice if you're going for something uncommon as not all flowers work well in bouquets. *Pictured right: Bouquet by Green Parlour.*

OTHER IDEAS

Dried flowers last forever and work really well for a rustic-themed wedding. Fabric flowers, made from wool, silk, felt, cotton, leather or pom-poms are a really tactile alternative to a real flower bouquet. Of course, you don't have to carry something bouquet-shaped at all. How about pin wheels or fans for a carnival-themed wedding? Balloons for something really playful, an amazing handbag or even an enormous lollipop? If you can carry it, it can be an alternative bouquet!

CENTREPIECES

Floral centrepieces are gorgeous and florists are an extremely talented bunch (boom boom!). A lot of time and labour go into creating beautiful floral displays, hence the cost. While I'd never disregard what an amazing florist can create, if having real flowers arranged by a professional isn't high on your list of priorities, then the good news is that there are lots of alternative things you can do yourself.

BUY WHOLESALE

If you're a DIY honey, then arguably the cheapest way to go about real flower centrepieces is buying the flowers wholesale and putting them together yourself. Buying blooms that are in season will likely be cheaper too. You can either get up at the crack of dawn and go to a flower market, or you can order them online (trianglenursery.co.uk is one of my favourites). Just be aware that you may need to order them a few days in advance to let them open up and give you time to put them all together. Even the simplest of arrangements – a few stems in a vase from a charity shop – can look really beautiful.

PLANTS

If you're keen to have some kind of living centrepiece, but for whatever reason you don't want cut flowers, then plants are your friend. Depending on the look you're going for, there are so many options too! Palm leaves and pineapples for a tropical theme, *monstera deliciosa* plants and macramé for an urban jungle feel, succulents and cacti for any occasion! You could use herbs in pots, which would add some fragrance too, or even just buy inexpensive bedding plants which you can plant in your garden afterwards. The best part of this idea is that they can be kept and used after the day, gifted to people who have really helped out with the wedding, or doubled up as favours for your guests to take away.

LIGHTING

Whether you just want to use a few arranged artfully on a mirror, or fill long tables with hundreds of the things, candles will give a really modern yet romantic feel to your tables. Be sure to check with your venue if you're allowed to have open flames and if not, consider using storm lanterns or hurricane vases with LED candles inside, or even lots of fairy lights, instead. Neon signs are increasingly popular and small ones can now be bought relatively cheaply at places like Paperchase and Sunnylife. Marquee lights and giant light-up letters also look really fantastic in photos.

CHECK OUT
Vowed and Amazed
Doris Loves
Bag and Bones
Love Inc

THEMED TABLES

If you're having a themed wedding, your centrepieces are where this will really shine. I've seen so many amazing examples of this, everything from tables themed around the seasons to holidays the couple have taken and movies where the poster artwork takes centre stage as the table marker. One of my favourite ideas for a Disney-themed wedding is naming each table around a different movie or princess and using different props to represent each one.

The key here is to plan each table carefully and start looking for props as soon as possible, because this will likely take some time! Scour eBay, Amazon, Target, supermarkets, Gumtree, Facebook Marketplace, HomeSense, TK Maxx (TJ Maxx), craft stores and charity shops… You never know where your next find may come from!

OTHER IDEAS

Pinterest is the key here, friends. A quick search for 'alternative wedding centrepieces' will bring up literally THOUSANDS of images and ideas you may never have even thought of. Here are some to get you started:

Kids' toys, stacks of books, birdcages, spray-painted dinosaur planters, pom poms on sticks, moss, skulls, photo frames, wooden stumps, mirrors, painted jam/kilner jars, fruit bowls, globes, balloons, feathers, teapots, vintage teacups, terrariums, pine cones, wheat, shells, drift wood, vintage typewriters, board games.

ENTERTAINMENT

There is an unbelievable list of options for entertainment at weddings, everything from your standard cheesy DJ all the way up to fire-breathers and burlesque performers! The right music and/or performers will kick your reception off with a bang and set the mood for the rest of the night, whereas even the most amazing wedding can fall flat if the DJ is a bit dodgy.

The things you choose will likely reflect the wedding theme and overall vibe you're going for – acoustic performers would be a lovely way to accompany you down the aisle if you're having an outdoorsy wedding for example, and a carnival or circus-themed day opens up a whole world of entertaining possibilities!

DJ

Undoubtedly one of the most popular forms of wedding entertainment is the classic wedding DJ. A great one will keep the party going all night long (or, at least until your venue kicks you out!). Listen to sample playlists before you book and let them know if there is a music style or any particular songs you categorically do not want to hear!

CHECK OUT
DiscoWed
The Wedding Smashers
The Best Men
Deckheds

PLAYLISTS

Of course, you could play DJ yourself and put together your own Spotify playlist. While it will certainly save you money, there is still something to be said about having a pro there who can read the room, make some crowd-pleasing selections you might not have thought of and take requests. If you are putting together your own playlist, you might want to have a few different ones – one for the drinks reception, one for the meal and another for the dancing… And if you're planning to have a heavy metal mosh-fest, you might want to save it until later in the evening when your granny has taken herself off to bed.

LIVE BAND

Neck and neck in popularity with a DJ would be having a live band, and for good reason: a great band will create a fantastic atmosphere and get people up and dancing. Make sure you think about where they'll be playing in relation to what else is happening at the time, though. If the band are in a different room to the bar, for example, they may end up playing to a nearly empty room, or if you're having a summer wedding with outdoor space to mingle, people may prefer to be outside in the evening rather than dancing inside.

It should go without saying, but make sure the band you hire are good! Ask if they have any YouTube videos of past performances, or even better, go and see them play in person. Also, remember that a band will probably take a few short breaks between their sets, which messes with the momentum, so make sure you have something else to fill the gaps.

CHECK OUT
Tailored Entertainment
Entertainment Nation
Warble Entertainment
Headliner

PHOTO BOOTH

I am yet to go to a wedding with a photo booth where it wasn't a huge hit. Everyone loves them, especially after a few drinks! Get one, get silly props and watch the madness unfold. You will not regret it.

CHECK OUT
Boxless Booths
The Photo Booth Guys
The Photo Emporium
Belle Studio

CIRCUS ACTS

Aerialists, fire-breathers, stilt walkers, jugglers, burlesque, drag or comedy performers – there are literally so many different ways to entertain your guests! There are even such things as living statues and tables – both weird and amazing in equal measure.

CHECK OUT
Alive Network
Sternberg Clarke
Circus Uncertainty
Circus Stardust Entertainment

OTHER IDEAS

Casino night, lookalikes, karaoke, singing waiters, magician, fireworks, solo singers, classical musicians, garden games, fairground rides, bouncy castle, caricaturist, bagpiper, selfie mirror, gospel choir, ceilidh band.

THE HEN PARTY & BRIDAL SHOWER

The hen or bachelorette party serves three main purposes: it's a chance for you to celebrate your friendship with your best babes, an occasion for you to be made to feel special and the time to get excited about the big day being right around the corner. It's also a chance for your closest friends from different friendship groups to meet. Bonding at a hen party makes the wedding so much more fun, especially for a fringe friend who may only know one or two people.

AN ALTERNATIVE HEN PARTY

In the UK, the hen party (bachelorette party in the US) is a rite of passage that usually involves copious amounts of alcohol, matching tee-shirts and/or sashes, maybe a stripper and the odd plastic willy straw. No judgement on anyone that wants to celebrate in this way, but there are also lots of alternative options for those of you who couldn't think of anything worse! Having a hen party abroad is an increasingly popular option, but of course it's also quite an expensive one... Here are some ideas to get you started if jetting off to Las Vegas or Ibiza is out of the question!

· Go for afternoon tea
· Spa day
· Sleepover/slumber party
· DIY cocktail making
· Visit a theme park
· Action/adventure activities
· Rent an AirBnB in the countryside
· Go to the zoo
· Play tourist in your own city
· Lush store party
· Crafternoon

Set a budget

One of the hardest things about organizing this is making sure that everyone can afford it. It can be really difficult to stick to a budget, especially when people have varying disposable incomes. As the bride, it's up to you to decide what is more important – that everyone you want to be there is, or that you do something more extravagant that maybe fewer people can attend. There's no right or wrong answer, this is your party! As a general rule in the UK, the 'hens' usually club together to cover the bride's costs, but it also depends on what you decide to do (asking them to cover flights might be a bit much!).

Start a Facebook or WhatsApp group

If your bridesmaids are organizing the party for you, encourage them to start a Facebook or WhatsApp group with everyone else in it to keep the communication going during the planning. (If you'll be cooking for yourselves, or booking restaurants, it's important that you check if anyone has any food allergies or dietary requirements so you can plan accordingly.)

Have an itinerary

If you have lots of things you want to do, schedule them at specific times and make sure everyone knows what's happening when. Don't forget to include time to recover from hangovers, have some chill time and get from A to B!

Delegate

A nice way to make everyone feel involved in the party is to give everyone a task. Whether that be going food shopping, cooking a meal, planning an activity or making games. This will mean the whole party isn't all on one person's shoulders and that everyone will feel invested in making it a really great event.

Make it extra special

It's the thoughtful little personal additions that make any hen party special, so pass this section over to your maid of honour to give her some ideas on how to make yours really memorable.

· Make everyone matching pyjamas or tee-shirts – it's so easy! Buy light-coloured, plain pyjamas or tee-shirts and transfer paper. Print photos

or text onto the transfer paper and iron on following the instructions.

· Ask each guest to bring a few photos featuring the bride to decorate the venue with. It's cheap, personal and a great conversation starter.

· Start the day with some games or ice breakers. Perhaps ask everyone to prepare their favourite story of the bride and take turns to share them.

· Write letters or well wishes for the bride to read the morning after the hen. Provide her with a beautiful box or scrapbook to keep them in.

· Ask each guest to bring a silly gift that reminds them of their friendship with the bride. She then has to guess who brought which gift!

· Be thoughtful with accessories —sashes and fluffy deely boppers aren't the only option!

Badges featuring each guest's name are a brilliant way to help identify everyone. Check out Oh Squirrel and Hard Felt Designs for well-made, quirky and non-cheesy options!

SO, WHAT IS A BRIDAL SHOWER THEN?

Bridal showers are very common in the US but the term isn't really used in the UK. In essence it's a gift-giving party held for a bride-to-be and generally a more formal and traditional event than a bachelorette party. It's usually a day-time gathering at someone's home. Even though they're not common in the UK, having a slightly tamer second event could be a nice way to include guests such as older family members who might not enjoy the activities planned for the main do.

the
CEREMONY

SAYING 'I DO'

HAVING THE CEREMONY YOU REALLY WANT

While dresses, decorations and flower displays are all very fun to think about and arrange, undeniably the most important part of any wedding is the ceremony. Ironically however, many couples leave it as a bit of an afterthought, assuming the legal bit is something they just have to get through before the party can begin. Actually, nothing could be further from the truth, and I'd say that of all the newlyweds I interview post-wedding, over 90 per cent of them say that the ceremony was their favourite part of the day, or that they didn't realize what a special and poignant moment it would be until they were actually there.

THE LEGALITIES

The laws surrounding getting hitched vary wildly depending on where in the world you are. In England, Wales and Northern Ireland you can only get married in a location consecrated for wedding ceremonies. The person performing the ceremony also has to be an authorized registrar or minister of religion. In Scotland, humanist and outdoor ceremonies are legal and in the United States, the laws are much more relaxed in general. The person marrying you is the one that gets the licence, rather than the location, meaning your best friend could legally marry you in your back garden if you wanted.

If you're planning to have a destination wedding or to marry abroad, the laws will vary depending on your chosen country. Be sure to do your research so that you understand what's going to be required of you. Not all marriages performed overseas will be legal when you return home.

DIFFERENT TYPES OF CEREMONY

Religious

If you have a strong faith, then you will most likely want a religious ceremony. With a focus on putting your faith at the centre of your relationship, the ceremony is officiated by a religious leader and incorporates the customs, traditions and rules of that faith, along with the legal requirements. A religious service can be held in a church, temple, mosque, synagogue or meeting room, and some clergy will officiate at non-religious sites too.

To have a Church of England wedding, you do not need to be a regular church-goer but you must make some kind of commitment to your chosen venue, whether that be through attending a marriage preparation course, giving notice of your intent to marry (having the banns read) and/or attending some services in the run up.

The majority of religions are licensed to conduct a wedding ceremony, which will also be legally binding, but some faiths (such as Pagan and Muslim) are not recognized under English law, so you may need to have a civil ceremony too. Catholic, Jewish and Quaker weddings are

more restrictive than Church of England and one, or both, of you must be baptized or a practicing member of the religion to be married in their places of worship.

I would say that having a religious ceremony should not just be about wanting to get married in a cool, old building. You will be making promises to God as well as each other, so it's important to consider if that's something you really want, or believe in.

Civil

If you don't want any reference to religion, then a civil ceremony might be for you. Civil ceremonies can take place at the register office/town hall or at any venue that holds a marriage licence. A civil ceremony follows a similar format to a church wedding, just without any spiritual or religious content. The songs you choose are also not allowed to reference God or religion in any way.

Celebrant-led

Often referred to as humanist ceremonies, interfaith blessings or a non-legal ceremony, celebrant-led ceremonies give you the most flexibility on how and where you get married. While they are legal in the US, Australia and Scotland, they are not yet recognized in England, Wales and Ireland. If you wish to have this type of ceremony you must also sign the necessary legal paperwork and declarations with

your local registrar. You could do this by going to the register office a few days before, or if your venue has a licence you could have a registrar attend and do this privately, before or after the non-legal blessing.

The options at a celebrant-led ceremony are endless and your celebrant will work with you to create a ceremony that feels right for the two of you. Handfasting, unity candle or wine ceremonies, ring warmings, a tree-planting ceremony and 'jumping the broom' are all options that your celebrant may offer.

UK ALTERNATIVE CELEBRANTS
· Alternative Ceremonies UK
· Inner World Outer Life
· The Celebrant Directory

US ALTERNATIVE CELEBRANTS
· Flora Pop
· The Reverend D
· XOXO, Jamelle

THE CEREMONY STRUCTURE

THE REHEARSAL

While a formal rehearsal dinner is commonplace in the US, for UK weddings the evening before will likely just be a casual gathering of your friends and family (or maybe a last-minute scramble to get all the DIY projects finished!). If you are having a religious ceremony you may be offered a ceremony run-through the day before. If you're using a celebrant or having a registrar come to your venue, they may offer it as an option as well, likely with an additional charge.

Although it might feel weird to be practicing getting married, it's actually a really good thing to do. The person leading your ceremony will talk you through everything that's going to happen and, if you want, give you the chance to practice your vows. If you don't have a formal rehearsal, at the very least it is a good idea to get a copy of the running order and everything that will be said before the wedding, so that you can rehearse and walk it through in private. This alone will help to make you feel more prepared.

I know for me personally, I actually really enjoyed our rehearsal. It was then that everything first started feeling very real and the enormity of what was about to happen really hit me! I cried throughout it, which actually turned out to be a good thing, too, because I got it out of my system meaning I didn't cry like a baby during the real thing!

THE REAL THING

Whatever type of ceremony you're having they usually follows a similar, basic structure.

· Processional (the bit where you walk in)
· Welcome by the officiant
· An address from the officiant about love or marriage (often referred to as the 'definition of marriage')
· Readings
· The declaration of intent (the 'I do!' bit!)
· Vows
· Ring exchange
· Pronouncement (the kiss!)
· The signing of the register
· Recessional (the bit where you walk out)

WRITING YOUR OWN VOWS

Unless you're having a religious ceremony where you may not be allowed to, writing your own vows is a really nice way to make the ceremony feel more personal.

There is so much information thrown about when it comes to vow-writing that it can all be a little daunting and overwhelming, but just remember that what really matters is the two of you and the commitment you are making. So, while listening to other people's advice, and Googling ideas of what to say is all well and good, the very best way to approach it is to simply speak from the heart and to be yourself.

A lot of people will tell you that you should consult each other to set the tone for your vows together, that if one of you is really emotional and the other is cracking jokes and referencing pop culture they won't work together. I don't agree with that idea personally. If anything, the words you choose to say SHOULD be unique to you as an individual. After all, a wedding is about two different people coming together and finding love. If one of you is a more emotional person and the other is sillier, then it's perfect that your vows would reflect this.

HOW TO BEGIN

If I'm feeling uninspired or stuck when I have to write, I find that just bashing out the bare bones of what I might want to say is a good way to lift the block. Start noting down words, phrases or bullet points of what you might want to say – remember that no one ever has to read it in this format. Once you get started and the words begin to flow, it'll be much easier to then go back and cut bits you don't like, flesh points out or fill in the blanks.

What to say

A nice basic structure is to cover your past, present and future and then make your partner a promise. Talk about how you met, when you first realized that you loved them, the things you've been through, how you feel about them today and what you hope for your marriage. Cover what being married to them means to you. Talk about your mutual obsessions and what defines you as a couple. Including references from your favourite movies, TV shows, video games or music is a lovely way to add some light relief and make them feel more personal.

Close with the promise you want to make them. Of course, you'll be promising to love them forever but how can you say this in a more unique way? Maybe you'll vow to always pick your dirty socks up off the bedroom floor, you'll continue to support their obsession with cosplay by going to every Comicon convention with them or you'll promise to make them an egg sandwich for breakfast every day. The more personal and intrinsically 'you two' the better.

Avoid clichés

You can borrow ideas from books or poems or even religious vows, but don't let someone else's words overpower what you really want to say. You want these words to sound like you and be meaningful to your relationship – after all, that's the whole point of deciding to write them yourself! Don't worry about being fancy or impressive – you don't have to be the most amazing writer for your vows to be really special. Remember, although your vows will be heard by other people, you are really only saying them for one other person's benefit – your new husband or wife.

Your vows should be about one to two minutes max. Pick the most important things you want to say and focus on those. You can always put some other personal thoughts into a letter for them to open as they're getting ready in the morning, or you can include them in a speech in the evening.

The ceremony and vows are such a vital part of the wedding so try not to leave them to the last minute. Also, don't stress about it – at the end of the day, this is simply your opportunity to tell your favourite person how much they mean to you. Your vows can be formal or they can be silly, they can be emotional or they can make your partner laugh out loud – ultimately, the choice is yours.

MUSIC & READINGS

Whatever type of ceremony you're having, the readings and music you choose are the most obvious ways to personalize the proceedings. While it's very easy for me to say 'just choose your favourites', it can be really difficult for some people to find ones they like, especially when it comes to readings.

You'll need about four song choices – one to walk into, one to leave by and a couple for when you're signing the register. The processional song is usually something slow and a bit more emotional (but it doesn't have to be!) and the recessional song would usually be more celebratory and uplifting.

PROCESSIONAL SONG IDEAS

November Rain – Guns N' Roses
Wedding Song – Yeah Yeah Yeahs (acoustic)
Marry Song – Band of Horses
Sea of Love – Cat Power
Songbird – Fleetwood Mac
First Day of My Life – Bright Eyes
Marry Me – Train
Always – Bon Jovi
Can't Help Falling In Love – Elvis Presley
You You You You You – The 6ths
Hearts Burst Into Fire – Bullet for my Valentine
Everlong – Foo Fighters
Heroes – David Bowie
Today – Smashing Pumpkins
Sweet Soul Sister – The Cult

Nothing Else Matters – Metallica
Strange and Beautiful – Aqualung
When the Right One Comes Along – Striking Matches
Jurassic Park theme – John Williams

RECESSIONAL SONG IDEAS

White Wedding – Billy Idol
Power of Love – Huey Lewis and The News
Everywhere – Fleetwood Mac
In My Life – The Beatles
Archie, Marry Me – Alvvays
You're My Best Friend – Queen
There is a Light That Never Goes Out – The Smiths
With Arms Outstretched – Rilo Kiley
I Believe in a Thing Called Love – The Darkness
Fell in Love with a Girl – The White Stripes
Stand by Me – Ben E King
All I Want is You – Barry Louise Polisar
You and Me Song – The Wannadies
You Make My Dreams – Daryl Hall & John Oates
Never Tear Us Apart – INXS
Friday I'm in Love – The Cure
Baby I Love You – The Ramones
Just Like Honey – The Jesus and Mary Chain
I Only Want To Be With You – Dusty Springfield
Star Wars (main theme) – John Williams

READINGS

Love manifests itself in lots of different ways – from the grandest of romantic gestures to the way she always boops your nose when you say goodnight. Just because you're wildly in love, doesn't mean you want to publicly express how you feel at every given moment. For this very reason, wedding readings can be tricky. It's way too easy to accidentally fall into clichéd choices because thinking about what you really want the readings to say is a bit cringe.

To help you get started, here are some of my favourite, lesser known options. Some are romantic, others are low key and more humorous. You could also use lyrics from your favourite love songs.

Let Me Put It This Way – Simon Armitage

Love – Roy Croft

The Amber Spyglass – Philip Pullman

He's Not Perfect – Bob Marley

Wild Awake – Hilary T. Smith

I Will Be Here – Steven Curtis Chapman

On Love – Thomas Kempis

I Wanna Be Yours – John Cooper Clarke

Falling in Love is Like Owning a Dog – Taylor Mali

Rings – Carol Ann Duffy

The Art of Marriage – Wilferd Arlan Peterson

The Life That I Have – Leo Marks

A Lovely Love Story – Edward Monkton

WEDDING TRADITIONS & FEMINISM

One of the more difficult realities you might come up against when planning your wedding, especially if you consider yourself a feminist, is just how patriarchal the original meanings of a lot of the traditions are. Everything from being given away (transferring of ownership from the father to the husband), throwing the bouquet (desperate women scrambling for their chance to be the next one to get married), even the way you cut the cake (woman feeds a piece to man first to signify her servitude to him) have uncomfortable origins.

HOWEVER, for me anyway, it's all about how you frame these traditions in your mind. The fantastic thing about planning an alternative wedding is that you can just do what makes you happy. I wholeheartedly encourage you to include, or adapt, any tradition that you want and ditch any you don't like.

BEING GIVEN AWAY

Asking your father to walk you down the aisle doesn't automatically make you anti-feminist. I know that for me personally, it was a really special moment between me and my dad. In no way did I feel owned by him, just as I do not feel owned by my husband now. For us, it felt like a really lovely symbolic gesture of the journey we'd taken together to get me to this point in my life and his acceptance of my husband into our family.

ALTERNATIVE OPTIONS

· Have both parents walk you down the aisle
· Have another family member or a friend walk with you
· Walk in on your own
· Come in with your fiancé
· Walk down the aisle alone and have your partner meet you halfway
· Take the journey to your ceremony with your dad, but walk down the aisle on your own

SEEING EACH OTHER BEFORE THE CEREMONY

This is more of a superstition than a tradition, but most couples choose to spend the night before the wedding apart and don't want to see each other before the ceremony. For some, this only adds to the excitement and anticipation, but for others it would feel weird not to wake up together on such an important day.

ALTERNATIVE OPTIONS

· Get ready and go to the ceremony together
· Wake up together, but get ready separately
· Wake up and get ready separately, but do a 'first look' before the ceremony

WEARING WHITE

Many people assume that the white wedding dress tradition is to do with symbolizing the bride's virginity, but this is actually completely false! Blue was originally seen as the virginal

colour (because of the Virgin Mary) and the white wedding gown only became popular after Queen Victoria wore one when she married Prince Albert in 1840. Before this, it was actually traditional for the bride to wear bright colours. The bigger and more colourful the dress, the richer and more powerful the bride's family was perceived to be.

ALTERNATIVE OPTIONS

· Wear your favourite colour!
· Opt for a jumpsuit or snazzy suit
· Choose a two-piece instead of a traditional gown
· Look to the high street/shopping mall for more affordable options
· Add non-traditional accessories to make your outfit feel more like you

THE RECEIVING LINE

The receiving line is a tradition where the newly married couple (and often their parents) stand and greet the guests as they arrive at the reception. The idea is that it provides the opportunity for the couple and their families to speak to every individual guest. However, this can be a very long and laborious process.

ALTERNATIVE OPTIONS

· Make a point of going around and saying hello to everyone during your drinks reception
· Visit each table between the courses of your wedding breakfast and say a few words to everyone

CUTTING THE CAKE

There are many different stories floating around about the wedding cake and the cutting tradition. Like with the dress, the larger and more extravagant the cake, the wealthier the bride's family was perceived to be. The bride feeding cake to her groom was supposed to signify her servitude to him (gross). Another theory is that fruit cake symbolized fertility and prosperity and so it was broken over the bride's head to bring good fortune to the couple.

ALTERNATIVE OPTIONS

· Choose a cake with flavours and a colour that both tie in with your wedding theme, rather than a traditional fruit cake
· Skip the big cake altogether and have a dessert table of different treats
· Have a completely alternative option instead of cake, such as a tower of donuts, wheels of cheese or pies!
· Forgo the formality of cutting the cake and ask your venue to cut and serve it as dessert instead

THROWING THE BOUQUET

This can be a really funny part of a wedding day (especially after a few drinks), but the sexist undertones are pretty disturbing. 'Come on single ladies, it's time to scrabble desperately for a bunch of wilted flowers because the victor will be the lucky one who snags a man next!'

ALTERNATIVE OPTIONS

· Include everyone in this moment – men, women, kids, married folks, singles…

· Don't throw the bouquet at all, keep it yourself and have it dried or in some other way preserved as a memento of the day

THE WEDDING PARTY

If you've always had a lot of friends of the opposite sex, why wouldn't you want to ask them to play such an important role? For some reason, many people assume that mixed wedding parties will ruffle a lot of feathers, but in reality, most people really won't be fazed at all and will probably think it's actually really cool that you chose to have all your best friends by your side, regardless of gender.

ALTERNATIVE OPTIONS

· Have a man of honour or a 'bridesman'
· Have a best woman
· Don't have bridesmaids or groomsmen at all
· Give the wedding party a rough guideline on the style of their outfits but let them make the final decision
· Instead of separate hen/stag (bachelorette/bachelor) parties, have a combined 'sten' do!

Ultimately, when it comes to wedding traditions, you should do what feels right for you and your relationship. The most important thing is that you make informed decisions on what you do or do not include in your day so that you end up having a celebration that feels authentic to you and your partner.

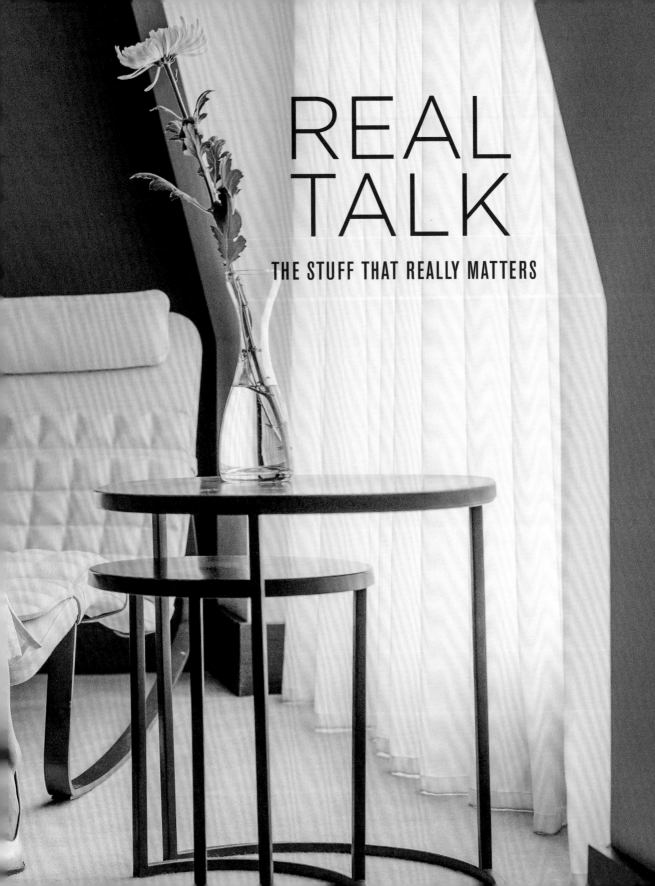

REAL TALK

THE STUFF THAT REALLY MATTERS

FAMILY DYNAMICS & WEDDING PLANNING

An impending wedding has a canny knack of bringing up lots of issues, emotions and difficult things that you might never have had to address before. Difficult family dynamics, keeping your feminist values aligned with your plans, not loving yourself or feeling worried about being the centre of attention – all of these things are frightfully common concerns. None of the things you struggle with on a daily basis magically disappear once you get a ring on your finger…if anything, they only get heightened!

FAMILY POLITICS, DRAMA & ARGUMENTS

Dealing with divorced parents, stressing about how one person might act, coping with meddling family members or just fretting about people not getting on are all typical worries. Is it any wonder there are entire reality shows centred around the drama of weddings (*Bridezillas* and *Don't Tell the Bride*, I'm looking at you!)?

I'm one of those lucky people whose parents are still together, and everyone in my immediate family likes each other. That being said, there were still difficult moments when planning our wedding. While I'm not going to sit here and claim to have all the answers (only you know how things tend to play out in your family), I do have some general advice for dealing with sticky situations that I hope might help.

It's not your job to please everybody

I have always been of the mindset that you can't please everyone, so you shouldn't waste your time trying. Yes, it can be a difficult thing to accept, but worrying about something you literally have no control over is nothing more than a massive waste of your time and energy. Worrying about something doesn't stop the fact that it may happen, it just means your mind is completely taken over by the possibility of it.

In an ideal world, everyone you love would just be so happy for you that they'd put their differences aside for one day… In an ideal world everyone would accept that this is your day and you should do the things that make you and your fiancé the happiest…. In an ideal world no one would have different opinions to your own…. But we all know this is far from an ideal world! People will bring their own issues, insecurities and priorities to the table because that's human nature. We're all intrinsically selfish, no matter whose day it's 'supposed' to be.

How you choose to protect yourself from these problems is all that matters. This is not about not concerning yourself with other people's feelings, of course you should do that, especially if the person in question means a great deal to you. But in some instances, you will simply need to accept that you can't keep everyone happy and you need to let it go. You may need to change your plans to keep things on an even keel or you may need to make some difficult choices.

Talk openly with potential troublemakers

In more practical terms, whatever the problem is, my advice would always be to try and speak openly to the people involved. Explain your concerns and let them explain theirs. You might realize that you were stressing about nothing, or you might be able to come to a decision that all parties are happy with. Compromise is always and will always be key.

See things from others' points of view

I've lost count of the number of times I've had brides say to me 'My mother/father/aunt/ sister is driving me mad! Why do they keep interfering? Why won't they just let us do things our way?'.

In these situations, it's important to take a step back to see it from all the angles. Put yourself in their shoes. Someone giving you unsolicited advice or seeming like they want to 'take control' is most likely their way of coping with everything that's going on, and for parents in particular, keeping their role intact. Sure, some people are just selfish and difficult, but in most instances the way they're behaving is probably a response to an underlying issue they're internally dealing with. If your bridesmaid is complaining about the choice of dress, what's more likely – that she's just being difficult for the sake of it or that she's feeling insecure about the way she might look in it?

This is especially true when it comes to parents. They have probably been thinking about the day you will get married since the moment your mother found out she was pregnant with you, so is it any wonder that they might want some involvement in how it plays out? Even if you find their ideas and suggestions frustrating, it is most likely just their way of feeling involved, needed and important. Realize that your mother's seemingly tactless comments may actually stem from her being over-anxious because she fears that things will go wrong. Try to understand and forgive her.

Families can be hard work and weddings can be massively stressful. Combine the two and for some people, it's a recipe for disaster. At the end of the day, you know the idiosyncrasies of your family, and you know how to best deal with them to protect yourself. All we can do is try our best and have faith that the people we love will be able to put their craziness aside for just one day. For the majority of you, I promise that they will, and for the select few amongst you that don't, well, at least you'll have an interesting story to tell your grandchildren!

CHILDREN AT WEDDINGS

You probably already know whether you really want to have children at your wedding or not, but it isn't always as straightforward as just doing what you want.

In the majority of cases, the decision will come down to your venue's capacity and your budget. Although many caterers offer children's meals, they're not always that much cheaper. A wedding can be a long day, so if you're having little ones you might want to think about bringing things in to entertain them too. Creating a dedicated safe play corner/den area with a pop-up tent decorated with fairy lights and filled with games and colouring books is a good low-cost option to keep them busy, but of course, whatever children's entertainment you choose will add to the overall cost in some way.

Opting to have a child-free wedding could cause friction between you and some of your guests but remember this is your day, you're paying for it and ultimately the decision is up to you.

Don't make any exceptions

The easiest way to deal with the issue is to have a blanket policy for everyone – it's either no children at all, or all the kids are invited. If you start making exceptions for some people it can get really messy and has the potential to cause upset and offence. You may well be met with resistance if you decide not to invite children, but the most important thing is to be consistent and treat everybody equally.

The only exceptions to the rule should be flower girls, ring bearers or your own children. Technically, they're considered part of the wedding party and don't violate an adults-only policy.

Make the invitations clear

Whether you are having children or not, your formal invitation is the place to make this clear. If kids are invited, make sure their names are also on the invite; if they're not, then you might want to call this out on your additional information card. A line saying something

like 'This is an adults-only event' should suffice but if you want to include an explanation you can always cite the venue choice or order of the day as not being child-friendly. It might also be a good idea to make a couple of phone calls (if necessary) to explain your position to anyone who you think will potentially have a problem with it.

Realize that some parents might choose not to attend because they simply won't be able (or won't want) to leave their kids at home. It's understandable and completely their prerogative, so don't be too upset if some people decline your invite because they can't bring their family with them.

TAKING CARE
OF YOURSELF

It can be difficult to even think about planning a wedding if you struggle with depression, anxiety or any kind of mental health problem. While choosing a dress, getting excited about flower arrangements and DIY-ing up a storm is all well and good, nothing is as important as looking after your own wellbeing.

If you're feeling daunted, then the likelihood is that it isn't the marriage that scares you, but the truckload of expectation surrounding the wedding itself. When you get engaged, you'll regularly be reminded that this should be 'the happiest time of your life' and people will automatically start asking you how the planning is going, but if you're finding things tough, this can only add to the pressure and feelings of failure. Not feeling good ALL THE TIME does not make you a 'bad bride', nor does it mean you shouldn't get married. The simple fact is that life goes on – just because you have a ring on your finger doesn't mean all your problems will automatically evaporate into thin air.

Even if it's not mental health you're dealing with – maybe work is stressful, your parents are getting divorced, someone you love is sick – whatever it is, this is real life, not a rom-com, and finding true love doesn't mean everything else is resolved and the end credits can roll.

Whatever your mental state, allow yourself to feel sad, give yourself the time you need to get things done and be kind to yourself.

Start small
If you look at the magnitude of tasks you have to complete in their entirety, you will only feel overwhelmed and unable to fathom ever getting it all done. I am very, very guilty of this. Break things down, tackle one task at a time and start small. Do some easier tasks first, something to help you get off the starting blocks and into the swing of things.

Do one thing every day that makes you feel good
This thing should not be in any way wedding related. Take some time as regularly as you can to do something that makes you feel more positive. And I'm not talking taking a bikram yoga class (unless that's your thing) or giving yourself 27 orgasms. I mean, take a bath, do a face mask, take your medication, have a friend around for a glass of wine, jump around your living room to a Britney Spears mega mix – small, manageable stuff that makes you feel good. The last thing you need is to add 'become a well-rounded-totally-got-my-shit-together-wonder-woman' to your gigantic to-do list.

Talk
Whether that be to your partner, your sister, your mum or a professional – just talk. Keeping feelings bottled up will ultimately only make you feel worse. I find that when I'm feeling stressed or overwhelmed about something, taking the time to vocalize it to someone who

cares will always make me feel so much better. Even if nothing has actually been resolved, getting out of my own head does wonders. Don't feel like you're burdening people either, if they love you, they'll want you to be happy and will be there for you if you need them.

Go your own way

If you've picked up this book, it's highly likely that doing your wedding your own way is up there on your list of priorities anyway, but if things are still feeling difficult, don't be afraid to throw the proverbial rule book (not this one!) out of the nearest open window.

Whether that be limiting the guest list so you don't feel anxious, choosing a venue that you feel safe in or wearing something non-traditional that makes you feel fabulous, DO IT. And if you are met with any resistance, then feel free to kindly remind people that your mental health is a priority and that this is how you'll feel the most comfortable on your day.

Don't feel the need to seek approval

Don't feel like you need to seek approval from everyone for all your ideas – you'll only be disappointed if you don't get it. Especially as an alternative bride, your taste will not be to everyone else's, and some well-meaning soul will probably advise against what you really want. When it comes to my fashion choices, for example, there is no way I'm asking my husband what he thinks. I love him, but he doesn't have my vision. If I want someone's opinion on my latest purchase, I'll ask my best friend instead! Keep some things to yourself, or only tell a select few, and surprise everyone else on the day.

Celebrate your achievements

It's important to remind yourself when you do a good thing, whether that be finally booking a supplier/vendor or just getting through the day. Write down your achievements each day/week/month. Keep them in a journal or even just on your phone, as long as it's somewhere they can be referred back to if you're having a hard time.

Treat yourself

I am a huge advocate of the 'treat yo'self' mentality and it doesn't have to be expensive. It could be as small as allowing yourself to spend a little money on something fun or it could just be allowing yourself time to watch a movie, take a long bath or curl up with a favourite book. You don't need to be on wedding planning duty 24/7.

Remember your wedding is only happening in the first place because you're so wonderful that another person proudly wants to show the world that you are their chosen person. They literally want to spend the rest of their life with you by their side. Put your mental health and your relationship at the forefront of any planning. Weddings are lovely, but those are the only things that really, truly matter.

WEIGHT LOSS & WEDDINGS

My relationship with food deteriorated when I was 14 years old. I went from being a healthy, happy child to a self-conscious teenager who thought she was fat and ugly and that being skinny would solve all her problems. I was on anti-depressants throughout most of my teens and early twenties, and in and out of treatment programmes for bulimia. Ironically, I only really started to recover when I got engaged.

So, you can imagine that the barrage of weight-loss 'advice' targeted at brides was an extremely difficult thing for me to navigate. Despite the body positivity community uprising, and a focus on inclusivity and diversity happening much more regularly, the wedding industry as a whole still constantly perpetuates the message that all brides-to-be must want to lose weight before their weddings.

I've seen and heard it all:

- Bridal shop owners asking girls if they plan to lose weight before their weddings and allowing them to order dresses that are way too small in order to 'slim into them'.
- Sample dresses more often than not only available to try on in smaller sizes.
- Mainstream wedding magazines with at least one article (or advertiser) dedicated to weight loss, whether that's through low-fat recipe ideas, exercise tips or even articles on pre-wedding plastic surgery.
- Wedding fairs with samples from diet companies in their goodie bags, as well as exhibitors offering everything from vibration plates you stand on while you exercise to punishing pre-wedding boot camps.

YOUR CHOICE

All of these things may seem relatively innocent on their own and weight loss businesses will cry that they're just responding to demand or giving people options, but the real issue is the reason why the demand is there in the first place.

Put all of the above together and the message is being broadcast loud and clear: losing weight for your wedding is not only acceptable, but expected, a requirement rather than a choice.

But you know what? IT IS A CHOICE – and it's yours to make.

I don't want to shame anyone who does choose to lose weight for their wedding. It's not for anyone, myself included, to dictate what you do with your body. For many, an upcoming wedding can be just the kick in their beautiful butt that they need to finally decide to start taking better care of themselves or making healthier choices. But it has to come from you, not the message that you're force-fed every day that you won't be happy until you fit into a smaller dress size.

Unfortunately, I don't see a big shift in attitude from the mainstream media anytime soon. The diet industry in the UK is worth close to £2 billion ($60 billion in the US) per annum

and although their messages might be packaged up and offered as happiness, beauty and health, ultimately, it's just about making cold hard cash.

A NEW ATTITUDE

So, as well as defying norms by choosing to wear Dr. Martens under our rainbow-coloured dresses, let's be revolutionaries in our attitude to this message too. I want this chapter to open your eyes a little and I want to propose an alternative option to anyone who feels that they need it.

This is your permission: YOU DO NOT HAVE TO LOSE WEIGHT FOR YOUR WEDDING.

You do not have to lose weight after your wedding either. Nor do you have to snap back into your skinny jeans a month after giving birth. You do not need to go on a crash diet to be beach body ready. Your body is already beach ready – have a body, go to the beach, achievement unlocked.

Listen to me: you are beautiful. You are a wondrous, unique and magical creature and there's no one else on this planet quite like you. You are worthy of love and you deserve to be getting married. Your fiancé loves you FOR YOU and your self-worth has absolutely nothing to do with the size label stitched inside your clothes, whether you have cellulite or not, or whether your belly is more wobble than washboard. Whether you're a size 4 or a size 34, you deserve to be loved, to be celebrated, to have a wedding that's filled with happiness, joy and a fucking enormous cake.

SHOULD YOU CHANGE YOUR NAME?

Kathryn Underwood was always last to be called in the school register, and it always bothered me (aren't the things that worry us as children so strange?). I always remember thinking to myself 'It's OK though, because when I get married I'll never have to be at the end of a register again…'

And then I married a Williams.

So, I guess you could say I always thought I'd change my name when I got married and even as a rebellious newly-engaged 23-year-old, who never, ever wanted to do anything that was expected of her, it never even crossed my mind that I wouldn't change it. For me personally, my surname didn't feel strongly linked to my identity, and changing it didn't ever feel like something I shouldn't want to do. I didn't dislike being an Underwood, but I never felt like it defined me. I defined me. I also decided that I wanted people to call me Kat instead of Kathryn when I was a teenager. I chose to be Kat, just as I chose to be a Williams.

But let's address the elephant in the room – does changing your name make you anti-feminist? I for one think it absolutely does not.

My decision to change my name had little to do with tradition or becoming my husband's possession, and more to do with just wanting a new name. I also liked the idea of us being like a team (in fact, we still call ourselves 'Team Williams' on occasion – I know, how sweet).

Kat Williams also just sounded super-cool, and in purely aesthetic terms I just preferred it! Victoria Beckham, Diane von Furstenberg, Beyoncé Knowles Carter and Amal Clooney all took their husbands' names, and I think you'll agree that they have to be some of the most successful, independent female entrepreneurs of our time.

But it all comes down to personal choice. I think the real feminist act is choosing to do whatever you want, and whatever makes you happiest – whether that be taking their name, them taking yours, hyphenating or even (as is getting more and more popular with alternative couples) making up a brand-new name for you both to take. This is your opportunity to call yourselves whatever you want, and that's a very powerful and exciting thing.

The American author and teacher Erica Jong once said, 'To name oneself is the first act of both the poet and the revolutionary. When we take away the right to an individual name, we symbolically take away the right to be an individual. Immigration officials did this to refugees; husbands routinely do it to wives.'

So, whether you decide to take their name, make up your own, or keep the one you were born with, knowing that you actually have the choice to call yourself whatever you want is the most important thing.

CAMERA CONFIDENCE

It's an innately British quality to hate having your picture taken, yet on your wedding day it's pretty unavoidable. I personally LOVE having moments captured, and being able to look back on them years later is such a wonderful thing. Plus, you always look back and realize you weren't as awkward as you thought you were at the time. Photographs are time capsules, so I'd hate for you to let your personal insecurities take that away from you.

My mum likes to bring out the old family photo albums when we all get together. I love looking back through them and laughing at my mother's giant hair, our questionable fashion choices, and the fact that my dad looked about 12 when I was born. My grandparents look young, happy and full of life and I look like the happiest baby that there ever was. It doesn't ever cross my mind to focus on anybody's 'flaws'.

Weddings are no different, and no matter what the magazines might tell you, your wedding day is not about being perfect – therefore neither are your photos. Sure, you might have a few portraits taken, but the vast majority of the photos from the day will be of natural things as they happen – the subtle smile your grandma makes when she gives you her vintage brooch to wear, the look on your fiancé's face as you walk down the aisle, the howls of laughter from your guests during the speeches – these are the moments you'll want to relive over and over. It's actually not all about you!

However, if you're still feeling nervous about being on camera, specifically about the more posed shots, here are some more practical tips.

Practice in front of the mirror
You'll feel ridiculous at the time, but move your body around to see how you look your best. A subtle flattering change of angle, the cocking of your hip, the raising or lowering of your chin, might be all you need to feel more confident.

Have an engagement shoot
If your photographer offers an engagement shoot, do it! Not only is it a lovely way to get some bonus photographs of the two of you, it is the perfect opportunity for you to practice in front of the camera AND get to know your photographer before the wedding day. Win-win!

Vocalize your concerns
Your photographer is not a mind-reader. If you are particularly self-conscious about something, then tell them! They might be able to suggest angles or poses to highlight your best assets.

You could also show them examples of photos of yourself that you like along with some inspirational shots of other brides with similar style. It's important that you're on the same wavelength, but also that you're realistic. If you are a voluptuous shape, don't expect them to make you look minuscule in the photos. Tell them if you need their guidance with posing.

NAILING A WEDDING SPEECH

The wedding speeches are a highlight of the day for many couples, but they are also one of the most traditionally patriarchal aspects of the event. I'm afraid the origin of this tradition is as disappointing as you might expect – men were seen as better at public speaking and the women were meant to just sit and look pretty.

This works out great for women who hate public speaking, but in the last few years more and more of us have decided to take the chance to say a few words too. In 2019 there doesn't seem a single reason for this not to happen.

Keep it short & sweet

On average, a wedding will have three speeches (father of the bride, groom and best man) so with 10 minutes each that's already half an hour. If the mother of the bride (or groom), the bride or bridesmaids are saying a few words too, that's another 30 minutes. People generally enjoy the speeches, but let's not push it. A few short, heartfelt words will go down way better than a rambling 45-minute lecture.

Include stories & anecdotes

Including stories is a great way to connect with an audience as people always relate to real-life anecdotes. Just be sensitive to the crowd, don't embarrass the couple (or your new spouse) too much – a light ribbing is OK but this is not the time to speak about that one time they (insert worst thing they ever did here).

Avoid the PowerPoint presentation

Best men listen up: no one wants to sit through your PowerPoint presentation. Leave it in the boardroom! If you must show embarrassing photos of the groom, get a couple of them printed out on large pieces of card instead.

Fake it 'til you make it

I am an out-and-proud show-off, an extrovert who loves nothing more than being the centre of attention, BUT until very recently public speaking was the one thing that made me really nervous. That was until I learned the magic 'fake it 'til you make it' secret. It sounds silly, but if you just pretend to be confident, people will have no reason to doubt that you're not.

Speak slowly and clearly, know your material inside out, smile and make eye contact with people in the audience. It really is as simple as that. If you still can't shake those nerves, remind yourself that IT'S ONLY TALKING – you've been doing it since you were two years old.

Don't worry about being perfect

The audience are on your side and they want you to do well. You do not need to be the slickest public speaker or have everyone howling with laughter. If you're not funny, don't try to force it. If you're a more emotional person, embrace it and don't be worried about shedding a few tears. Take a few moments to speak from the heart and it will be totally fine, I promise.

AVOIDING POST-WEDDING BLUES

The post-wedding blues are very real and something many newlyweds tell me they feel intensively once the day is over. I've been there too – in fact, I got them so bad that 12 years later I'm STILL writing about weddings!

It's hardly surprising though – this day you've been tirelessly planning and obsessing over, the event that all evenings and weekends for the past year have been taken over by, all that plotting and crafting and dreaming about what the day itself will actually be like… suddenly it's all over. You might even feel a bit depressed about not being a bride or groom anymore, or maybe you're simply wondering what you'll do now to fill your time.

Don't feel guilty about being sad

If you're anything like me, the planning of your wedding was a huge, life-changing experience, and anything that's been such a big a part of your life is going to be a bit difficult to let go. Feeling a bit sad that it's all over does not make you any less happy to be married and it certainly doesn't make you a bad person. Allow yourself to be blue for a while, but then pick yourself up and make the effort to get over it! Wallowing in your sadness will only perpetuate it, so start making strides to move on to your next adventure.

Don't have wedding regrets

No wedding day goes completely perfectly. Looking back and thinking 'Oh I wish we'd done this' or 'What if we'd done that?' will only make you feel worse. You made the decisions for your wedding that were right for you at the time.

Have something to look forward to

When things feel a bit sucky, it's always nice to have something coming up that you're looking forward to. Whether that be as big as your honeymoon or starting a family, or as small as a date night or repainting the hallway – think of all the free time you'll have now you're not planning a wedding! What have you always wanted to do?

Keep in touch with your wedding buddies

Maybe you made some new friends in a wedding planning Facebook group, or there's a girl at work that you always used to chat to about wedding planning because she was engaged too? I think it's really good to have people around you that are at a similar life stage as you. It's great to have friends at different points in their lives too, but if you're the only one who's married you might start to feel a bit alienated and wish you were 'free and single' like them. Obviously, you shouldn't be breaking ties with your old friends now you're hitched, but why not add some new ones to your inner circle?

Remember, this is the beginning not the end!

After all, the purpose of having a wedding is to get married, so even if you occasionally feel a bit sad that you're no longer engaged, don't forget what the wedding was all about in the first place! The wedding was a big fabulous party to celebrate the two of you promising to spend the rest of your lives together. Don't feel like you have to slip into old married couple stereotypes. Do things to keep your relationship fresh and exciting – have date nights, plan trips, start new hobbies, spend time with your friends. Nothing has to change unless you want it to.

While there's no doubt that getting married and planning the most awesome party you can is really, really fun, I promise you that actually being married to your favourite person in the world is way better!

REAL
WEDDINGS

HOW REAL COUPLES PLANNED THEIR UNIQUE CELEBRATIONS

MEXICAN FIESTA MEETS COUNTRY HERITAGE

Holly and Steven's first holiday together was to Mexico, so they wanted to bring the colour and fun of that vacation into their wedding.

Holly and Steven were married at Buckland Hall near Brecon, south Wales. The contrast of the traditional venue with their colourful, quirky theme worked really well and made their day feel personal to them. 'We didn't follow tradition for a lot of things', Holly says. 'We wanted to put our own personalities into every aspect which made it quite unique! We hired a Bucking Bronco as entertainment in the evening – this went down so well with all of our guests, young and old!'

The craft projects were plentiful, especially when it came to the decorations. 'We handmade Mexican matchboxes for our favours and filled them with candies. This was inspired by a Frida Kahlo matchbox brought back from Mexico. We also spray-painted traditional donkey piñatas gold for our centrepieces – this was fun, quick and looked effective!' The pops of colour were continued in their floral arrangements.

Holly wore a traditional dress and veil, but when paired with her beautiful tattoos and rose gold hair, her bridal look ended up being quite edgy. 'A funny moment was when I walked down the aisle', she recalls. 'We had decorated the beautiful stairway with paper star lanterns, but didn't take the width of my train into account, so I ended up with half the lanterns tangled up under my dress and all its layers!'

'We handmade
Mexican matchboxes
for our favours
and filled them with
candies. This was
inspired by a Frida
Kahlo matchbox
we brought back
from Mexico.'

Photography: Kirsty Mackenzie Photography
Wedding planner: Sylvie and Joan
Venue: Buckland Hall
Bride's dress: Pronovias
Bridesmaid dresses: Kelsey Rose
Flowers: Flowers by Becca Jane
Cake: Epic Cakes

ELEGANT GOTHIC CASTLE WEDDING

Bunny and Michael's castle wedding was edgy and gothic in style, yet still glamorous and totally gorgeous.

Even though it looks like it could be nestled in mysterious Transylvania, the venue chosen by this couple was the glorious Hempstead House in New York. 'We fell in love with this venue', explains Bunny, 'and there was no doubt we were ready to do what it took to have it. Our theme was high fashion couture with a gothic fantasy twist. I couldn't see my wedding taking place at a typical venue. I wanted something that was true to what we both liked.'

Bunny wore the most spectacular sheer-backed figure-hugging black wedding dress by Galia Lahav, 'I've seen maybe a handful of other brides wear black, but I wear black every day and couldn't see myself getting married in any other colour. I don't regret it one bit.' Her dark and delightful flower headpiece also brought serious regal vibes to the look in a deliciously deep colour palette.

To keep those fantasy elements alive (Bunny and Michael met at a pop/geek culture convention in 2003), they picked a song from *Game of Thrones* for their wedding party to walk down the aisle to, and then another for Bunny's arrival. 'I wanted a dramatic entrance and I think I achieved it', she says. 'Everyone kept telling me their jaws hit the floor! We kept things simple after that, as we wrote our own vows and I wrote the ceremony script. I wanted to keep things light-hearted and easy, with a little bit of humour.'

The bride used her graphic design background to plan their reception décor to perfection. They opted to keep things on theme with centrepieces of tall cylindrical vases filled with water, deep purple orchids and floating candles. 'Seeing it all come together was the best thing about planning our wedding. I won't lie, I found it very stressful, so whenever a vendor was paid for, or flowers etc. were chosen, I got excited. It meant one less thing to worry about, and meant we were getting closer to the day!'

'I've seen maybe a handful of other brides wear black, but I wear black every day and couldn't see myself getting married in any other colour.'

Photography: Mike Zawadzki Photography
Venue: Hempstead House, New York
Bride's dress: Galia Lahav
Flowers: Arcadia Floral Company

A BUDGET-FRIENDLY WEDDING WITH RAINBOWS, UNICORNS & GLITTER

With a budget of less than £4000, Natalie and Daley planned a unique and colourful celebration right in the heart of London.

Our wedding theme was rainbows, unicorns, glitter… and Prince!' says Natalie. 'We combined love of travel, music, food, colours and glitter. We wanted the wedding to reflect everything we love since it was essentially a day about our love.'

The ceremony at London's Islington Town Hall was full of tears and laughter from everyone. 'The registrar accidentally called Daley "Mr" (which we were fine with as Daley is non-binary) and everyone erupted in laughter which really brought us down to earth.'

To keep costs down, the couple made all the reception décor and props, bought their outfits online and took the train (with all 50 of their guests!) between the ceremony and reception. 'We thought it would be really funny to get the train to the reception together… All 50 of us. At rush hour. On a Friday. It was as mental as you'd imagine but surprisingly we managed to only lose two guests on the platform – that's pretty impressive, right?! On the way to the station tons of people were taking photos and saying "Congratulations!", it felt like we were famous! Then, when we got on the train, we all had a little singalong to random songs. It was totally amazing.'

One of the most important things to this pair was including their friends and family. They all pitched in to help create the wedding of their dreams. 'Our wedding was really held together by our friends and family', Natalie explains. 'The craft nights to make all the decorations, the artwork for stationery, even the bunting was gifted to us by friends. We couldn't decide on a cake flavour or how much cake to buy so we had our very own Great British Bake Off (minus Mary Berry) and about five of our friends baked cakes and got super competitive about it! It was a really nice, chilled out day – even during the planning we were pretty relaxed.'

'We combined
love of travel, music,
food, colours and
glitter. We wanted
the wedding to
reflect everything
we love since it was
essentially a day
about our love.'

Photography: Clare Tam-Im
Ceremony venue: Islington Town Hall
Reception venue: Hatch, Homerton
Natalie's dress: ieie Bridal
Natalie's shoes: Iron Fist
Daley's outfit: ASOS
Stationery: Sofie Birkin & Each Peach Studios

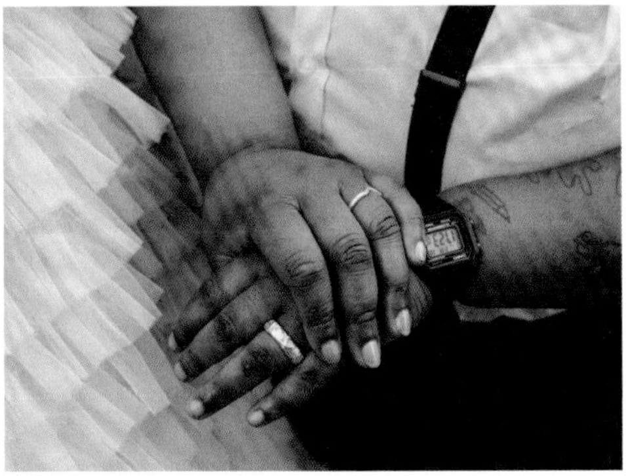

"THE DALEY"
Strawberry Bourbon Cobbler
"THE NATALIE"
Blueberry Mojito

MENU
JERK CHICKEN • BURGERS • CURRY GOAT
VEGGIE & HALLOUMI SKEWERS
SWEET POTATO & CHICKPEA CURRY
RICE & PEAS • MAC & CHEESE
PLANTAIN • CARIBBEAN BREAD • SALAD
BURGER BUNS • COLESLAW
CHECK DIETARY REQUIREMENTS WITH SERVERS
original artwork by

ROCKABILLY
VIVA LAS VEGAS

Dafna and Eylonzo live in Israel but with the bride working
in the wedding industry as a make-up artist, they wanted
to do something different for their own celebration.

The decision was made to fly to Las Vegas for a pop-up ceremony on a rooftop officiated by female Elvis! The creative bride made her own dress and veil and put together her bouquet. She also did her own hair and make-up.

They timed their wedding so they could also attend Viva Las Vegas Rockabilly Weekend at the same time. 'As we were flying over to attend the festival, we decided to seize the opportunity and elope', the bride explains. 'We plan to throw a party for all our family and friends this winter in Tel Aviv, but this was our chance to have an intimate fun ceremony.'

One of the most important things to them was getting great wedding photographs, so this influenced their choice of ceremony. 'In Las Vegas it is quite common for wedding chapels not to allow an outside photographer – they want you to book the photographer they provide. As much as we envisioned the classic Vegas chapel wedding, for us the photography was more important. Thanks to our photographers we got in touch with Florapop and discovered Holly was working on a new ceremony as a female Elvis impersonator! We were psyched. We both envisioned an Elvis officiant, but are both feminist and wanted a woman to officiate. We also both love drag so this was the perfect option for us!'

'We're happy with how everything went and we are left with super cool memories. When you don't plan every little detail, you allow yourself to be surprised. We followed our hearts and our love.'

Photography: Pure Light Creative
Officiant: Florapop

LOVE IN SAN FRANCISCO

Joey and Chie were married at the stunning Conservatory of Flowers, located in Golden Gate Park.

The overall look of the wedding was influenced by Chie and Joey's playful nature and love of bright colours. 'We're all about disco balls, sparkles, video games and dinosaurs!', says the bride. 'Our theme was kind of modern chic. We wanted things colourful and fun, but to keep that hint of fanciness.'

To add a handmade touch, Chie created invitations, wine labels and menus. Joey home-brewed a batch of beer as gifts – he even designed personal labels and bottle openers! 'There were so many awesome parts to the wedding', Chie remembers, 'but my favourite moment has to be a tie between the awesome LED-light lion dance and the officiant speech by Joey's brother-in-law. Having him leading our ceremony made it feel so personal and special. He really set the tone for the night ahead.'

'Our theme was kind of modern chic. We wanted things colourful and fun, but to keep that hint of fanciness.'

Photography: Steve Cowell Photography
Wedding planner: The Love Riot
Venue: Conservatory of Flowers, San Francisco, CA
Bride's dress: Chi Chi London
Flowers: Studio Choo Florists

URBAN EAST LONDON WEDDING

Hannah and Chris didn't want their wedding to feel themed, but they were massively inspired by the venue where their day took place.

The couple both love where they live in east London so this was the jumping-off point for all the decisions. 'I don't feel we had a specific theme!' Hannah begins. 'We wanted it to be very urban and very London and venue-wise we knew we wanted a warehouse feel, so plenty of exposed brickwork was important, along with festoon lighting. We also wanted to make sure we incorporated landmarks such as London buses, street signs and graffiti into our photos.'

The bride wore a two-piece from Emma Beaumont, a bespoke dressmaker based in Cheshire, changing the skirt in the evening to a feathered one found on eBay for just £35! 'I knew I wanted separates. I'd seen loads on Pinterest and I'm not keen on traditional wedding dresses – I feel more comfortable in skirts and crop tops. I was also really keen on a comfy outfit change for the night as I knew how much I wanted to party.' Her bridesmaids looked just as stylish in black dresses of their own choosing from various high-street shops.

They hosted their reception at the super cool Shoreditch Studios, a perfect space for a laidback, urban feel. It also didn't need a lot of extra decoration, which suited this casual couple. 'We made a massive BAR sign which we painted gold, sourced vintage tea chests to use as tables and added white bunting.'

'Lighting was really important to us so we had festoon lights in the ceremony and reception arch, along with plenty of uplighters, and a giant disco ball in the reception arch.'

Photography: Lisa Jane
Photography
Ceremony: Arch 1, London
Reception Venue: Shoreditch
Studios, London
Bride's dress: Emma Beaumont
Groom's attire: French Connection
Flowers: Edie Rose Designs

ECLECTIC & COLOURFUL WEDDING IN CHILE

Cata and Manu's wedding was a perfect blend of everything they love, from animal masks and fortune cookies to temporary tattoos.

Getting married in a beautiful country like Chile meant that Cata and Manu were inspired by everything around them. They wanted a day that felt like them but also played homage to their home. 'Our wedding was a mix of lots of things we like', explains the bride. 'We had lots of fun animal masks for people to wear, fortune cookies with personalized messages as favours and temporary tattoos for people to play with.' The outdoor setting provided the perfect informal background.

Their simple civil ceremony was the highlight of the day for them both. 'It was an intimate ceremony and very simple, with a special song and so many people that we love there with us. It was perfect and we'd change nothing about it. We loved our wedding!'

'The ceremony
was perfect and
we'd change nothing
about it. We loved
our wedding!'

Photography: Blanco Rios
Wedding planner, cake & flowers:
Amelia Lamas Banqueteriá
Venue: Casona Linderos, Buin,
Chile
Bride's dress: ASOS

SNAZZY SUITS, SEQUINS & ALL THE CONFETTI

Gemma's 'Suits and Sequins' summary of her London wedding to Guy is very apt, as in true Sinatra style they did things their way.

Their Peckham wedding was emotional and incredible from start to finish, from that sparkly green wedding dress to the 'Silly Old Beans' sign they were married under. 'There wasn't a straight-up inspiration for the wedding,' explains Gemma, whose day job is working in events. 'With any event I plan, I can find that really restrictive, and the beauty of a wedding is that you don't have to have those boundaries. It can just be about you two, even if nobody else "gets it". Having said that, we did ask everyone to dress in suits and sequins, and it was amazing how everyone turned up – the best dressed bunch of wonderful people.'

They decided not to have any flowers as Gemma wanted a really synthetic look instead, opting for glitter, lights and sequins. She used plastic instead of plants, describing it as a 'Vegas approach'. The reception, held at the Peckham Liberal Club, was decked out in light bulbs and sequins as well, and the invites went out in mirrored gold envelopes filled with sequins.

This Vegas approach continued to the décor, which Gemma wanted to make as much of as possible. 'I'm training myself to sign-write and lots of the time we spend walking around together as a couple is punctuated by diversions for signs I've always wanted to snap. I knew that would play a part in the look.' Their pretty unique sign wording is courtesy of their engagement. 'We got engaged at Festival No. 6, which was gorgeous, but we weren't that sober! We didn't really have a "family-friendly" engagement story until we got back to the hotel. Guy is a prolific sleeptalker but what he was saying that night was completely new, including "What's the worst that can happen? She's such a safe pair of hands" and "We are such silly old beans, ah, silly old beans". I thought this was super cute and so the signs for the decorations all became based on things Guy said in his sleep!'

The marriage of...

Gemma Pharo &
Guy Parsons

October 29, 2016

SILLY OLD BEANS

'I'm training myself to sign-write and lots of time walking around together is punctuated by diversions for signs I've always wanted to snap. I knew that would play a part in the look.'

Photography: Devlin Photos
Ceremony venue: Asylum Chapel
Reception venue: Peckham Liberal Club
Bride's dress: Nadia Tahari
Bridesmaid dresses & groom's suit: ASOS

RUSTIC CHARM MEETS RETRO SASS

The wedding of Samantha and Ross was an accumulation of their own personal styles mixed with rural British countryside charm.

Samantha and Ross wanted their wedding to be reflective of their personal day-to-day aesthetic. 'My style is very 40s & 50s vintage, so this also inspired my wedding day look', Sam explains. 'The bridesmaid dresses were based upon the same era and the dressmaker even made a mini custom version for our daughter, Betty. I'm a country music fan, which worked well with our location and is why we had lots of hessian and rustic touches. Ross is into 70s trojan music and has a massive love of ska and reggae, so we used our favourite bands as table names and we had our guests find their table by looking for the correct vinyl artwork.'

The ceremony was the bride's favourite moment of the day. Her mother walked her down the aisle. 'I was given away by my mum and we walked down the aisle to Marvin Gaye's *How Sweet it is (to be Loved by You)*. It was a wonderful feeling to see Ross at the end of the aisle waiting for me and the look he gave me when he saw me – I knew he would cry! We chose a poem by John Cooper Clarke titled *I Wanna Be Yours*, instead of doing our own vows as we are both quite nervous of public speaking. We walked off with our little girl in tow to our song, *Do I Love You* by Frank Wilson.

Their venue, Hunters Hall in Norfolk, stylistically already suited their rustic, countryside-themed wedding so they didn't need to do much in terms of extra décor. However, they did make a few things themselves. 'We kept our décor relatively low key. My sister organized a photo display of Polaroid photos of us, all presented on a huge wooden frame with flowers at the top. We hired some simple glass jars and wood slices from our florist to decorate our tables. We also made our own wedding favours, buying the sweets in bulk and bagging them and labelling them ourselves.'

We kept our decor
relatively low key.
My sister organized
a photo display of
Polaroid photos of us,
all presented on a
huge wooden frame
with flowers at the top.

Photography: Camilla Andrea Photography

Venue: Hunters Hall, Norfolk

Bride's dress: Chotronette

Groom's attire: Adam of London

Bridesmaid dresses: She's Dynamite

Cake: Constance Rose Cakes

Flowers: Libby Ferris Flowers

FAERIE & WOODLAND NYMPH FANTASY WEDDING

This one-of-a-kind celebration for Mackenzie
and Morgan took place at Sacred Mountain Ranch
in Julian, California.

Their theme was an autumn fantasy woodland wedding. 'Think *Lord of The Rings*, fairies and satyrs', says Mackenzie. 'It was also LARP (Live Action Role Playing) inspired. We actually had a sword duel during the reception dinner.'

All of their cosplay-loving friends got seriously into the fantasy theme spirit, too. 'We wanted to join all the parts of our lives together, from our biological family to our LARP family. Our biological family had never experienced LARP, so we brought it to them. Most of our friends are also LARPers and work in the film industry so of course we had to have a high fantasy Live Action Role Play costumed wedding.'

The wedding party had a whimsical fairy wonderland feel as well, with the bridesmaids and groomsmen all dressed as forest nymphs and centaurs. 'We homemade the costumes for the bridal party as well as the ring bearer costume, flower girl costume and the fathers. Some of the bridesmaids helped sew the costumes as well.'

'We homemade the costumes for the bridal party as well as the ring bearer costume, flower girl costume and the fathers.'

Photography: Pink Feather Photography
Venue: Sacred Mountain Ranch, Julian, CA
Mackenzie's dress: Jusere
Morgan's dress: ieie Bridal

Welcome
to
The Wedding of
Morgan
and
Mackenzie

Please pick a seat
not a side, you are loved
by both brides

PHOTOGRAPHY CREDITS

COMMISSIONED PHOTOGRAPHY:

CREATIVE DIRECTION
Kat Williams
rocknrollbride.com

PHOTOGRAPHY
Devlin Photos
devlinphotos.co.uk

PHOTOGRAPHY ASSISTANTS
Lisa Jane Photography
lisajane-photography.com and
Lee Allen Photography
leeallenphotography.com

STYLING
The Bijou Bride
thebijoubride.com and
Mr and Mrs Unique
mrandmrsunique.co.uk

HAIR
Love Hair & Co.
lovehair.co.uk

MAKE-UP
Louise Seymour
louiseseymour.co.uk

CREATIVE ASSISTANT
Sophie Cooke
crownandglory.co.uk

RUNNER
Ellie Kime
theweddingenthusiast.co.uk

LOCATIONS
South Place Hotel
southplacehotel.com and
JJ Studios
jjmedia.com

Front cover
Eric Ronald ericronald.net

Back cover
Janneke Storm jannekestorm.com

Endpages
Lisa Jane Photography
lisajane-photography.com

The author and publishers would like to thank the following photographers for allowing us to use their beautiful images in this book:

UK
Amy Faith Photography
amyfaithphotography.com 70, 103,

Camera Hannah
camerahannah.co.uk 4, 5b, 7b, 8–9, 36–37, 79, 93a, 93c 106–109

Camilla Andrea Photography
camillaandrea.com 192–197

Candid and Frank
candidandfrankphotography.com 40–41, 74b, 74c

Clare Tam-Im Photography
claretamim.co.uk 152–157

Costa Sister Productions
costasisterproductions.co.uk 95

Devlin Photos
devlinphotos.co.uk 5a, 17b, 19a, 19c, 42–43, 45, 50–55, 59, 73, 76–77, 81, 83, 88–89, 96–99, 100–101, 116–117, 131, 132, 184–191

Epic Love Story
epiclovestory.co.uk 35

Jeanie Jean Photography
jeaniejean.com 69al

Kirsty Mackenzie Photography
kirstymackenziephotography.co.uk 125, 138–143

Lee Allen Photography
leeallenphotography.com 21

Lisa Jane Photography
lisajane-photography.com 1, 3, 6, 19b, 49, 58, 61–65, 86–87, 127, 170–175

Marni V Photography
marnivphotography.co.uk 105

Miss Gen Photography
missgen.com 135

Peppermint Love Photography
peppermintlovephotography.com 38a, 38b, 69ar

Rob Dodsworth Photography
robdodsworth.co.uk 31–32, 38c, 68

US
Aimlee Photography
aimleephotography.com 113, 114br

Anna Lee Media
annaleemedia.com 25, 30, 69bl, 72, 104

Hazelwood Photography
hazelwoodphoto.com 71, 74a

James Westray
jameswestray.com 10–11, 12

Mike Zawadzki Photography
mikezawadzki.com 144–151

Pink Feather Photography
pinkfeatherphotography.com 136–137, 198–203

Pure Light Creative
purelightcreative.com 158–163

Samm Blake Weddings
sammblakeweddings.com 17c, 69br, 114al

Steve Cowell Photo
stevecowellphoto.com 164–169

Two Foxes Photography
twofoxesphotography.com 17a, 24, 28–29

Yaritza Colon Photography
yaritzacolon.com 33, 93b

EUROPE
Blanco Rios
blancoriosfoto.com 92, 176–183

People Truelove Tellers
peopleproducciones.com 26–27, 111, 121

AUSTRALIA
Eric Ronald
ericronald.net 5cr, 85

Janneke Storm
jannekestorm.com 2, 13

Talitha Crawford Photography
talithacrawfordphotography.com 5cl, 67, 119

Tricia King Photography triciaking com.au 75, 91

SUPPLIERS

The author and publishers would like to thank the following suppliers for loan of their items for the commissioned photography in this book:

CLOTHING
Beyond Bridal
beyondbridal.co.uk

Chotronette
chotronette.com

E&W Couture
eandwcouture.co.uk

Grace Loves Lace
graceloveslace.com.au

Honeypie Boutique
honeypieboutique.co.uk

Legends Bridal
legendbridaldesigns.co.uk

Lucy Can't Dance
lucycantdance.com

Rembo Styling
rembo-styling.com via

Halo & Wren Bridal
haloandwrenbridal.com

Sharon Bowen-Dryden
bowendryden.co.uk

The Couture Company
the-couture-company.co.uk

Laurie Lee Leather
shoplaurielee.com

SHOES & ACCESSORIES
AM Faulkner
annmariefaulkner.co.uk

Faith via ASOS
asos.com

Florence Shoes
iamflorence.co.uk via
Woburn Bridal
woburnbridal.com

Free People
freepeople.com

Irregular Choice via
RIOT Lounge
riotlounge.co.uk

Naturae Design
naturaedesign.com

Rock n Rose
rocknrose.co.uk

VEILS & HEADPIECES
AM Faulkner
annmariefaulkner.co.uk

Beyond Bridal
beyondbridal.co.uk

Crown and Glory
crownandglory.co.uk

Rachel Webb
instagram.com/rachellunawebb

Mcfayden Millinery
mcfaydenmillinery.com

Rock n Rose
rocknrose.co.uk

BOUQUETS
Beaubuttons
beaubuttons.co.uk

Crown and Glory
crownandglory.co.uk

Green Parlour
greenparlour.com

May Contain Glitter
maycontainglitter.com

CAKES & TOPPERS
Blossom and Crumb
blossomandcrumb.co.uk

Gaya's Cakes
gayascakes.com

Rachel Emma Studio
etsy.com/shop/RachelEmmaStudio

Tattooed Bakers
tattooedbakers.com

STATIONERY
Papier x Disney
papier.com

Wedfest
wedfest.co

Sailor and Scout
sailorandscout.com

Veronica Dearly
veronicadearly.com

HEN/BACHELORETTE PARTY
Oh Squirrel
ohsquirrel.co.uk

NEON LIGHTING
Vowed and Amazed
vowedandamazed.co.uk

INDEX